# THE MUSIC DIRECTOR'S COOKBOOK
## Creative Recipes for a Successful Program

Published by
Meredith Music Publications
a division of G.W. Music, Inc.
4899 Lerch Creek Ct., Galesville, MD 20765
http://www.meredithmusic.com

Cover and text design by Shawn Girsberger

Copyright © 2005 MEREDITH MUSIC PUBLICATIONS
International Copyright Secured • All Rights Reserved
First Edition
July 2005

International Standard Book Number: 1-57463-039-3
Library of Congress Control Number: 2005928326
Printed and bound in U.S.A.

# Contents

# Foreword

The idea for this collection came about while I was perusing a cookbook that my wife received as a Christmas gift. I was impressed with the design, layout, and above all, the excellent recipes that seemed to celebrate delicious, healthy food. While reading, I was suddenly inspired to create a similar "cookbook" for music directors, with each recipe providing a suggestion for increasing one's own knowledge or for improving a performance ensemble. As the thought developed, I realized that I would need knowledgeable and experienced music educators to assist me with this project—individuals who had proven themselves to be excellent musician-educators. And so I began the task of selecting those individuals whom I knew fit this criteria and could provide unique and motivational ideas and concepts.

The subject for each recipe was left up to the individual. A "passion for the topic" was the only requirement. Although the topics turned out to be quite varied, a number of them are based on the selection of literature—perhaps an indication of the need in this area. The fifty-seven authors that were selected are all experienced music educators, composers, or authors who have developed superb programs, or have otherwise excelled in our field, providing guidance and outstanding musical learning opportunities for thousands of student musicians. Their collective wisdom is beyond measure, as is their generosity. Each writer is donating the royalties that they would have earned on this project to the American Music Conference (AMC), a non-profit affiliate of NAMM, the International Music Products Association. Through their proactive approach, the American Music Conference leads the way in support of music education in America and around the world.

The concepts presented in this publication range from philosophical to practical and will surely motivate the reader to continue in the pursuit of personal growth and the acquisition of further knowledge. It is my hope that these "recipes" will be read with an inquisitive mind, embracing the many outstanding ideas presented.

*Bon appetit.*

Garwood Whaley

# Acknowledgments

To each of the *chefs* who contributed to this publication, I offer my sincere thanks. Each individual responded to my initial invitation by telephone with a resounding "yes." They were each enthusiastic about being involved in what they felt would be a unique and worthwhile contribution to music education. Their generosity has been exceptional, their expertise unquestionable, and their love of music and music education inspiring. The writings within, presented by them, are based on years of study and experience from a variety of educational and professional levels.

Thanks to Bruce Bush of the Hal Leonard Corporation for our many discussions about this project and his continued encouragement during its production. To Shawn Girsberger, my unending gratitude for her work with Meredith Music Publications and for the artistic layout and cover design of this volume. A special thanks to Peter Boonshaft and Fred Harris for suggesting several writers with whom I had no prior acquaintance. For leading the way in support of music education in our schools and for their assistance in marketing, thanks to Joe Lamond, President and CEO of NAMM, and Laura Johnson, Associate Executive Director of the American Music Conference. I would also like to offer my sincere appreciation to the many individuals who have encouraged me throughout my career as a writer and publisher.

And finally, to the thousands of music students and their directors who have inspired each of us, our never-ending thanks for your dedication, beautiful music making, and the belief that music does make a difference.

Garwood Whaley
President/Owner
Meredith Music Publications

# About the Authors

**Mark Aldrich** is Professor of Music at Salem State College in Salem, Massachusetts, where he teaches courses in music technology, conducts the concert band, and is music director/conductor of a new professional ensemble on Boston's North Shore, "Salem Winds." He holds a degree in music education from Keene State College (B.M.), and degrees in instrumental conducting from the University of Massachusetts/Amherst (M.M.), and the University of Colorado/Boulder (D.M.A.).

**Kenneth Amis,** after obtaining a masters degree in composition, became the tuba player of the Empire Brass in 1993. Mr. Amis has served on the faculties of Boston University, Boston University Tanglewood Institute, the Royal Academy of Music, Lynn University, Pacific Music Festival, and Massachusetts Institute of Technology. He has been commissioned by numerous organizations, including the College Band Directors National Association, and his many works are published by Boosey and Hawkes Inc. and Amis Musical Circle.

**Terry Austin** is Director of Bands and Professor of Music at Virginia Commonwealth University. He lives in Richmond with his wife Tracia and his twin sons Joshua and Seth.

**Frank L. Battisti** is Conductor Emeritus of the New England Conservatory Wind Ensemble, the Massachusetts Youth Wind Ensemble, the Tanglewood Institute's Young Artists Wind Ensemble, as well as Principal Guest Conductor of the Longy School of Music Chamber Winds. He has appeared as a guest conductor, clinician, and educator throughout the United States and the world. He has had numerous articles on conducting/music education and the wind band/ensemble published in national and international journals and magazines.

**Jay Bocook**, widely in demand as composer, arranger, conductor, and educator, has contributed compositions and arrangements to the opening and closing ceremonies at the 1984 Olympic Games and provided music for the Olympic Games in 1988, 1996, and the 2002 Winter Games in Salt Lake City. Since 1989, he has been an exclusive composer for the Hal Leonard Corporation and, in 2000, was appointed Director of Athletic Bands at Furman University in Greenville, South Carolina, a position he currently holds.

**Peter Loel Boonshaft**, author of *Teaching Music with Passion*, is currently Professor of Music, Director of Bands, and Director of the Graduate Wind Conducting Program at Hofstra University in Hempstead, New York. Dr. Boonshaft holds Bachelor of Music (Summa Cum Laude), Master of Music Education in Conducting, and Doctor of Musical Arts degrees.

**Lynn M. Brinckmeyer**, Professor of Music, is Associate Chair of the Department of Music at Eastern Washington University. Her degrees include a Bachelor of Science in Education and Master of Music Education from Eastern New Mexico University, and a Ph.D. in Music Education from the University of Kansas. Dr. Brinckmeyer directs the Concert Choir and Opera Workshop at Eastern Washington University. She recently began serving as National President-Elect for MENC, the National Association of Music Education.

**Michael Burch-Pesses** is Director of Bands at Pacific University, where he conducts the wind ensemble and jazz band, and teaches conducting, music education, and MIDI technology. He enjoyed a distinguished career as bandmaster in the United States Navy, serving as senior bandmaster and head of the Navy music program. Under his direction, the Naval Academy Band received the George Howard Citation of Musical Excellence from the John Philip Sousa Foundation, the highest civilian award for a military band.

**Charles F. Campbell, Jr.** is a member of the American Bandmasters Association, a high school representative for the National Band Association, and a member of the Bands of America Advisory Board. During his thirty years as a high school band director, his groups have received the John Philip Sousa Sudler Shield and Sudler Flag of Honor, and two of his three bands have performed at the Midwest Clinic.

**John E. Casagrande** retired as Director of Bands at W. T. Woodson High School in Fairfax County, Virginia after serving in that capacity for eighteen years. Prior to that position, he served as Director of Bands at Ambler (Penn.) Junior High School, East Stroudsburg (Penn.) High School, and Mount Vernon (Virginia) High School. He currently teaches music education courses at George Mason University in Fairfax, Virginia.

**Reber Clark** is a composer and former music educator working in the Chicago area. His work is published worldwide by C. Alan Publications, Wingert-Jones Music, and Southern Music Company. He is a graduate of Arkansas Tech University and studied composition with James Perry.

**James Cochran**, one of the world's leading authorities on wind music, holds bachelors and masters degrees in clarinet and conducting from Southern Illinois University-Edwardsville. Since 1974, he has been employed by Shattinger Music, where he has counseled and advised wind band conductors on repertoire for thirty years.

**Michael Colgrass** is a Pulitzer Prize-winning composer who has also written a number of works for young band. Recently, he has developed a system for teaching children and music teachers how to create music.

**Gary Corcoran** has been Professor of Music and Director of Bands in the Department of Music, Theatre, and Dance at Plymouth State University in Plymouth, New Hampshire since 1991. Dr. Corcoran has held similar positions at Pittsburg State University in Kansas and Georgia State University in Atlanta, having taught previously in the public schools of Maine and Massachusetts.

**Paula A. Crider**, Professor Emeritus, University of Texas, has taught at all levels. She is a past president of the National Band Association, and was recognized as the 2004 Texas Bandmaster of the Year.

**Thomas C. Duffy**, D.M.A., is Deputy of the School of Music and, since 1982, Director of Bands at Yale University. He is an active composer and writes music that generally embraces extramusical programs and social issues.

**Cheryl Floyd** is Director of Bands for the nationally acclaimed Hill Country Middle School band program in Austin, Texas. She is a recognized authority on middle school band pedagogy and for two decades has actively sought commissions to create significant new works for the middle school band.

**Richard Floyd** has served as Texas State Director of Music at the University of Texas in Austin and holds the post of Artistic Director and Conductor of the Austin Symphonic Band. Floyd has toured extensively throughout the United States, Canada, Australia, and Europe as a clinician, adjudicator, and conductor.

**Eileen Fraedrich** is the author of *The Art of Elementary Band Directing* (Meredith Music, 1997) and has taught in Fairfax County, Virginia since 1984. She received her Bachelor of Music degree, summa cum laude, from Ithaca College and her Master of Arts degree from George Mason University

**Rob Franzblau** serves as Associate Professor of Music and Director of Bands at Rhode Island College, where he conducts the wind ensemble and chamber winds, and teaches courses in music education at the graduate and undergraduate levels. He is the founder and conductor of the Rhode Island Wind Orchestra, a chamber wind ensemble of professional musicians.

**David C. Fullmer** is Assistant Professor of Music at Utah Valley State College (Orem), where he conducts the symphony orchestra, jazz ensemble, and percussion ensemble. He is also Director of Bands at Timpview High School and President of the Utah Music Educators Association. He earned B.M. and M.M. degrees from Brigham Young University and a D.M.A. in Instrumental Conducting from the University of Washington, Seattle.

**David R. Gillingham** is Professor of Music Composition at Central Michigan University. His works for band and percussion have earned him an international reputation. Over sixty of his works for band, choir, percussion, chamber ensembles, and solo instruments are published by C. Alan, Hal Leonard, Southern Music, MMB, T.U.B.A, I.T.A., and Dorn.

**Steven Grimo** is presently serving for the USAF Bands and Music Branch as Commander of the USAF Academy Band, in Colorado Springs, Colorado. A graduate of the New England Conservatory of Music, he was awarded the Doctor of Musical Arts degree in Conducting from Catholic University of America.

**Alan Gumm** is a Professor of Music Education at Central Michigan University and a researcher and author on the topics of music teaching style, motivation, learning style, and perception. He graduated from McPherson College and received a Masters of Music from Fort Hays State University and a Doctor of Philosophy in Music from the University of Utah.

**Frederick Harris, Jr.** is Director of Wind Ensembles at Massachusetts Institute of Technology, where he serves as Music Director of the MIT Wind Ensemble and MIT Festival Jazz Ensemble. Dr. Harris earned the Master of Music degree from New England Conservatory and a Ph.D. from the University of Minnesota. He has commissioned over 50 works for wind and jazz ensemble.

**Samuel R. Hazo** is the only composer in history to be awarded the winner of both composition contests sponsored by the National Band Association. He is presently under contract with the Hal Leonard Corporation. In addition to composing, Mr. Hazo is a music educator in the Upper St. Clair School District, where twice he has been honored as "Teacher of Distinction" by the Teacher's Excellence Foundation of Southwestern Pennsylvania.

**Leslie W. Hicken** is director of the wind ensemble, symphonic band, and chamber winds at Furman University, where he also teaches instrumental conducting, instrumental music education, and is assistant to the marching band. He received his Bachelor of Music degree from the Eastman School of Music, Master of Arts in Teaching from Columbia University, and Doctor of Music Education from Indiana University.

**Roy C. Holder** has been working in public school music education in Tennessee, Georgia, and Virginia for the past thirty-five years. He is currently Director of Bands at Lake Braddock Secondary School, where his ensemble has performed at the Virginia Music Educators Association Conference, the Midwest Band and Orchestra Clinic, and the American Bandmasters Association Convention.

**Shelley Jagow** is director of the Wright State University Symphonic Band and Saxophone Quartets, and professor of saxophone and music education courses. She earned Music Education degrees from the University of Saskatchewan and the University of Missouri, and received a Ph. D. at the Union Institute & University, where Colonel Timothy Foley, Frank Battisti, and Edward Wingard served as her mentors.

**William Jastrow** is a member of the Neuqua Valley High School Music Department (Naperville, Illinois), a contributing author on percussion education for the Percussive Arts Society, and a past Band Division Vice President and State President of the Illinois Music Educators Association. He holds a Bachelor of Science degree in Music Education from the University of Illinois and a Masters of Music Education from Northwestern University.

**Barry E. Kopetz** is Director of Bands and Professor of Conducting at Capital University, where he conducts the symphonic winds and the wind symphony. He received his bachelor and master degrees from Ohio State University and holds a doctorate with distinction from Indiana University. Kopetz is active as a composer and arranger, with more than seventy published works. In 1997, he was selected as "Utah Music Educator of the Year" for his work contributing to the growth and quality of the instrumental music programs in the state of Utah.

**Kenneth Laudermilch** is Professor of Instrumental Music and Director of the Wind Ensemble and Chamber Winds at West Chester University, Pennsylvania. He earned his master's degree from the New England Conservatory of Music and his Doctor of Musical Arts degree from Catholic University of America.

**Tim Lautzenheiser** is President of Attitude Concepts for Today, Inc. He also serves as Executive Director of Education for Conn-Selmer, Inc., and he is a nationally recognized advocate for music in our schools.

**Edward S. Lisk** is an internationally recognized clinician, conductor, and author. A graduate of Syracuse University School of Music, he has served as an adjunct professor, clinician/lecturer, adjudicator, and guest conductor throughout forty-five states, five Canadian provinces, and Australia. He is an inducted member of the American Bandmasters Association and in the year 2000, served as the sixty-third president of this distinguished organization founded by Edwin Franko Goldman.

**Mitchell Lutch** is Visiting Instructor of Music and Director of Bands at Central College in Pella, Iowa. He is also nearing completion of a Doctor of Musical Arts degree in instrumental conducting from the University of Washington. After receiving his Master of Music degree from the New England Conservatory of Music in 1990, he taught high school instrumental music for twelve years in New York State, during which time he served as president of the New York State Band Directors Association from 1997–1999.

**Matthew McInturf** is the Director of Bands at Sam Houston State University. He previously taught at Florida International University and in the public schools of Richardson, Texas.

**Allan McMurray** is Distinguished Professor, Robert and Judy Charles Professor of Conducting, and Director of Bands at the University of Colorado, a position he has held since 1978. Considered a leader in conductor education, he is author of a series of DVDs on instrumental conducting, and annually hosts the College Band Directors National Association Conducting Symposium.

**Charlie Menghini** is President and Director of Bands at VanderCook College of Music in Chicago, Illinois. He is co-author of the Hal Leonard *Essential Elements 2000 Band Method* and a contributing editor for *The Instrumentalist* magazine.

**Stephen W. Miles** is the Instrumental Music Specialist for the Baltimore County Public Schools and the conductor of the Baltimore Music Educators Wind Symphony, in Maryland. He is a graduate of Shenandoah Conservatory of Music and the University of South Carolina.

**Linda R. Moorhouse** is Associate Director of Bands at Louisiana State University, President of the National Band Association, past President of the Women Band Directors International, and is a Member Laureate of Sigma Alpha Iota. An elected member of the American Bandmasters Association, she graduated from the University of Florida, Louisiana State University, and is a degree candidate at the University of Washington.

**Willis M. Rapp** is Chair of the Department of Music at Kutztown University, where he serves as conductor of the university orchestra and Director of Percussion Studies. He holds Bachelor's and Master's degrees in Music Education from West Chester University, the Diploma in Fine Arts in Wind Conducting from the University of Calgary, and the Doctor of Musical Arts in Instrumental Conducting from Catholic University of America.

**Jeffrey Renshaw** is the conductor of the wind ensemble, chamber orchestra, and new music ensemble at the University of Connecticut. He also coordinates the graduate conducting program.

**Nathalie Robinson** is an Assistant Professor and Director of both undergraduate and graduate music education programs at Hofstra University. She has more than fifteen years music teaching experience at the elementary and middle school levels. She is extremely active as a guest speaker and clinician at state, regional, and national conferences. Recently Dr. Robinson served as a visiting professor at the Cultural University of Taipei, Taiwan.

**Timothy Salzman** is Professor of Music and a Donald E. Petersen Endowed Research Fellow at the University of Washington, where he serves as Director of Concert Bands and is conductor of the University Wind Ensemble. Over his twenty-seven year career, he has been a conductor, adjudicator, or arranger for bands in over thirty-five states, Canada, England, Japan, South Korea, Indonesia, Thailand, and Russia and currently serves as compiling editor and co-author of *A Composer's Insight: Thoughts, Analysis and Commentary on Contemporary Masterpieces for Wind Band.*

**Deborah Sheldon,** with degrees from Mansfield University, Penn State University, and a Ph.D. in Music Education from Florida State University, is Associate Professor of Music Education at Temple University. Her specialties include assessment, band literature, conducting, curriculum development, music psychology, rehearsal methods, and research. She has authored numerous articles, texts, and performance materials for band. Sheldon taught elementary and secondary instrumental music in Pennsylvania and New York and has served as guest conductor throughout the United States.

**Thomas E. Slabaugh, II** is currently a doctoral student at the University of Washington, studying instrumental conducting with Tim Salzman and Peter Eros. He holds degrees from California State University, Sacramento and has taught in public school and collegiate music programs throughout Northern California.

**Frederick Speck** is Director of Bands at the University of Louisville, where in addition to his work with the ensembles, he teaches composition and conducting. His music is published by C. Alan and others.

**Lawrence Stoffel** is Director of Bands and Conductor of Wind Ensembles at California State University, Northridge (Los Angeles). He earned the Doctor of Music degree from the Indiana University School of Music.

**Carl Strommen** has a B.A. in English literature from Long Island University, an M.A. in music from the City College of New York, and has studied arranging and orchestration at the Eastman School of Music. He is an Adjunct Professor of orchestration, arranging, and composition at C.W. Post College in Brookville, New York. His publishers include Warner Bros., Alfred, Carl Fischer, Boosey & Hawkes, Shawnee Press, Heritage Press, and Smart Charts (jazz band).

**James Swearingen** is Professor of Music and Department Chair of Music Education at Capital University located in Columbus, Ohio. With over four hundred publications, his numerous compositions for band reflect a variety of musical forms and styles that have been enthusiastically received by school directors, student performers, and audiences worldwide.

**John A. Thomson** is Director of Bands at New Trier High School in Winnetka, Illinois, and a consulting editor and new music reviewer for *The Instrumentalist* magazine. His degrees are from Carnegie Mellon University and Northwestern University.

**Johnnie Vinson** is Director of Bands and Professor of Music at Auburn University, where he has been a member of the faculty since 1969. With over three hundred works, he is also a widely recognized arranger/composer of music for band.

**Barry Ward** teaches in the Diocese of Arlington, Virginia Schools, where his four elementary and middle schools have a combined enrollment of over five hundred students. He is the conductor of the Bishop Ireton High School Concert Band, performs professionally with the Arlington Symphony, and maintains a private clarinet studio. His concert band compositions are published by C. Alan Publications.

**Renee Westlake** is the Music Supervisor in Bozeman, Montana and was the Northwest Division MENC president from 2003–2005. She taught advanced placement music theory, world music, band, and general music for twenty-six years before moving into administration. Renee lives on a fourth-generation wheat and barley farm in a mountain valley near Yellowstone Park.

**Garwood Whaley** is president of Meredith Music Publications, Conductor Emeritus of the Bishop Ireton Wind Ensemble, and past president of the Percussive Arts Society. He graduated from the Juilliard School of Music and received a Doctor of Musical Arts degree from Catholic University of America while performing with the United States Army Band, "Pershing's Own."

**Carol Zeisler** is in her twentieth year as a middle school band director and is currently at Northside Middle School in Norfolk, Virginia. She plays principal oboe in the Virginia Wind Symphony.

**Dennis Zeisler** is in his twenty-sixth year at Old Dominion University, where he is Chair of the Department of Music, Director of Bands, and Professor of Clarinet and Conducting. Mr. Zeisler is Conductor of the Virginia Wind Symphony, an adult wind group based in Norfolk, Virginia.

# Saliferous Silence

*Mark Aldrich*

A Down Easter's definition of salt: "It's what makes the potatoes taste flat when there ain't any." The same might be said about sound without silence. Although not usually intended as the dominant flavor, salt and silence, when used in balance and moderation, will enhance most other flavors.

**INGREDIENTS**
None.

**SERVES:**
Ensemble musicians and their conductors.

### As a basic flavor
Silence is the only element of musical ensemble performance that depends on every member to create. Silence is, therefore, surprisingly rare and more difficult to obtain than one might imagine. When used effectively, silence itself is as interesting, compelling, or dramatic as any sound it enhances.

### As a flavor enhancer
Detached articulations, or silences between sounds, can give any musical line distinction, even in a dense, contrapuntal texture. Accuracy is required from everyone to perform the silences in a staccato line. A single, insensitive player or singer could destroy the efforts of many by sustaining longer, indiscriminate note lengths. Silence must be performed with intention.

Syncopation is most often thought of as accenting sounds on weak pulse subdivisions, but in many cases, it could be thought of as actively asserting silences on strong pulses. In these cases, syncopation relies on both elements; each is dependent on the other for effect.

Occasionally concentrating on silence rather than sound can bring variety to any interpretation. While preparing a standard march for an obligatory performance and looking for a fresh perspective to offer, a conductor asked the ensemble members to actively perform the score's twenty, single-beat, ensemble rests. The piece sparkled.

### In raising
Extending an ensemble's expressive range should be accomplished not only by raising the dynamic ceiling but also by lowering the floor. As dynamic levels approach silence and the

1

dynamic range becomes narrow, the responsibility of individuals to control their sound within that range becomes more and more critical. An ensemble can only perform as quietly as the least sensitive member of the group will allow.

A section leader performing a pianissimo tone (60 dB) could be joined by nine section members, all performing that tone at that level, before their perceived loudness would double to piano (70 dB). By impractical extension (other than massed bands or choirs), they could then be joined by ninety more section members before their loudness would again double to mezzo piano (80 dB). However, one insensitive or self-asserting member in the section, imposing a mezzo forte (90 dB) by themselves, would negate the efforts of everyone by raising the section's perceived loudness level to their own.

Humans respond to changes in sensory stimulus, often alternating between two extremes. Regarding loudness, we respond to changes in sound pressure levels ranging from sounds that verge on physical discomfort (118 dB) near one extreme, to silence (0 dB) at the other. For optimal expression, an ensemble's controlled performance range should be expanded in both directions, to safely include as much of that hearing range as possible.

**In clarifying**
Imagine your last rehearsal or performance, and that you could somehow silence all of the intended, musical sounds. What would you still hear? Keys and valves clicking, feet shuffling and tapping, performers gasping for air, water being blown out of tone holes and tubing, sticks and mutes dropping, chairs creaking, pages fluttering, talking . . . could you add anything to the list? Or more importantly, could you take anything away? A common misconception is that these non-musical noises are covered and are thereby rendered inaudible by the louder musical performance.

Performing music into silence might be likened to brushing watercolors onto a clean canvas. And a smudged canvas, like a noisy environment, always shows through. Although a fundamental tone may comparably overpower its harmonics, the still-audible presence of those harmonics contributes timbre to the sound. In a similar manner, masking many extraneous noises with a louder musical sound may cause them to recede into the background by comparison, but they still contribute an audibly indistinct, "muddy" quality to the overall sound. Great care should be taken to initially create, and as far as possible, maintain a silent environment during rehearsals and performances.

**For a tasteful finish**
A focus on sound brings our attention first to the manner in which sound begins. The progressive order of sound in time, its beginning, duration, and end, has been taught to us since childhood. From our earliest music teachers and method books we learned how to start a sound, then how to sustain it, and then, perhaps receiving less attention by default, how to stop it. Teacher/conductors often give most of their energy to initiating sounds, and only if there are no immediate entrances to cue, to expressing a line's contour or shaping its release. Young musicians unfortunately learn by example that starting a sound is more important than finishing it. When we concentrate on silence rather than sound, we think and respond oppositely. A focus on silence brings our attention first to the manner in which silence begins its crescendo if you will, with the release of sounds—after all, music's final impression. ➤●

# All Music Begins with a Good Breath (and Dies with a Lack Thereof)

*Kenneth Amis*

Ask any brass or woodwind student or band director what the most important aspect of playing a wind instrument is and most will respond that it is the ability to effectively use one's air. Ask them to estimate how much breathing and air control contribute to good wind playing and most will concede a figure over 70 percent. Ask how many of them practice breathing on a daily basis and you'll be amazed at how few actually do. This lack of correspondence would almost be humorous if not for the fact that it is so limiting to the development of the performers and, by extension, the music they make.

**INGREDIENTS:**
Ensure that everyone does daily breathing exercises. Provide constant and consistent visual encouragement from the podium for good breathing. Install a sense of responsibility in players to breath as a team. Use metaphors that lead performers to think of airflow and how it relates to timbre, rather than just decibel levels.

**SERVES:**
All brass and woodwind players.

At a certain level of professional development, all the players in an ensemble will arrive at rehearsals and performances completely warmed up, both aerobically and muscularly. Unfortunately, this usually does not occur until the collegiate level and, even then, only in the most studious and competitive environments. This situation creates a major problem for a conductor who wishes to tighten rhythms, hone intonation and balance, and create dynamic phrasing. These issues depend on reliable articulation, supported tone production, and flexible tone manipulation. All of these prerequisites stem from good breathing—both inhalation and exhalation—and the body must be prepared to undertake the act of good breathing as it relates to the instrument in the player's hand.

Some school schedules will offer a time for wind players to congregate before their daily rehearsals to do breathing exercises. For those of you without this convenience, I highly recommend that you do the following breathing exercise with your students before every rehearsal and performance. Some of you may be reluctant to lose time from your rehearsal for such personal maintenance. However, given the importance of good breathing to everything you are planning to do, this time will be more than made up in productivity. It is of vital importance for larger instruments and for when you have early morning rehearsals or meet in cold environments.

Here is a simple exercise that only takes 2½ minutes. With all your woodwind and brass players seated, have them inhale for a full 8 seconds, hold their breath for 24 seconds, exhale for a full 8 seconds, and then relax for 10 seconds. Complete this exercise three times, for a total of 150 seconds. Your percussionists can be setting up during this time, and you can make quick announcements during the 10-second relaxation periods. Be sure to count, or have one or your percussionists count, the seconds aloud so that the participants learn to associate breathing with time and rhythm. This exercise will help to stretch out the muscles around the ribs and chest to accommodate deeper breathing and will quietly calm and focus your ensemble in preparation for work.

Provide constant visual encouragement for good breathing. An ensemble that breathes together plays together. This includes the conductor. Be sure to show a good inhalation before every entrance that you cue. The breath should be measured (from one to four beats long, depending on tempo) and always be obvious and musically encouraging. You can usually tell if a group will play its first note together by hearing if it breathes together.

During a performance, not all entrances are cued from the podium. Each section leader should be made aware that it is his or her personal responsibility to bring their section in with a good, metered breath, even when the section is cued by the conductor. The other members of the section should be made aware that their first responsibility is, when technically appropriate, to breath with their section leader, even when they are cued by the conductor. This will develop a strong sense of team, with a clear hierarchy—e.g., the second and third trombones follow the principal trombone player's lead, who follows the principal trumpet player's lead, who follows the conductor's lead. You'll find that ensemble problems are much more easily solved when each section functions as a unit. The first step to this unity is learning to breathe as a section.

During a piece, the section leader should show, at least, the two beats before a section entrance. The first beat is shown with something like a downward motion or soft, short grunt, and the second beat—the one before playing commences—with an obvious, rhythmic breath. This will reassert the tempo to section members and give them the confidence to come in together.

Using simple verbal instructions all the time, such as "louder" or "softer," can often lead young players to both misunderstand why they are being asked to do so and misconstrue what they need to do to accomplish it. The novice and intermediate player will often correlate "louder" with a misguided sense of muscular forcefulness and "softer" with a lack of presence and breathing. Mix in descriptions that spark the imagination and encourage the movement of air. For instance, instead of saying, "This section should be much louder," you can say, "We need our biggest and warmest sound to blossom throughout the room." Or, instead of repeatedly telling them to play softer, you can tell them to "send a whisper to the other end of the auditorium." Instructions such as these will not only make you more interesting to listen to but will also engage a part of a young player's brain that is less likely to get trapped in the misconceptions and anxieties of technique.

There are no quick fixes for the idiomatic problems shared by wind groups. However, the process for overcoming these problems, and so many others in life, begins by first taking a *deep breath.* ➤•

# Enhancing Expressiveness through Accurate Dynamic Placement

*Terry Austin*

Achieving good dynamic contrast is a goal of all conductors. Many ensembles, however, do not give as much attention to placing dynamics as they give to other aspects of their playing. As a result, many ensembles do not play with the expressive impact that they could otherwise have.

**INGREDIENTS:**
Any piece of music that includes dynamic markings. This can also be done using scale exercises with dynamics indicated by the conductor.

**SERVES:**
All instrumental and voice students.

One of the most immediately apparent aspects of musical performance is dynamic contrast. Most ensembles attempt to make dynamic contrast, even if other fundamentals are lacking. Even if dynamic contrasts are achieved, they will not contribute appreciably to the overall expressiveness of the performance if they are not done with the same intensity, the same shape, and in the same place. It is very important that everyone in your ensemble agrees on these points.

Dynamics take two basic forms. The first is sudden changes in dynamic such as a change in one beat or less from forte to piano. The other is gradual increases or decreases of intensity over a period of time (crescendo and diminuendo). In the first case, it is important for your students to know precisely where the change in dynamic occurs. Everyone needs to make the change of dynamic at the same time. I often find that young players approach dynamics a little like some of us do speed limit signs. As soon as we can see it, we change speeds. Dynamics cannot be effectively done that way. Composers write dynamics to highlight certain notes, or specific sections, and to shape phrases. If we do not put the emphasis at those precise moments, expressiveness is lost. It is also important that everyone agrees on the intensity of the change. All fortes are not alike.

Try this. When encountering dynamic changes for the first time, stop the ensemble and practice the resulting dynamic. Adjust the balance and intensity until you feel that it is what you want to achieve at that moment. Then back up a few measures and practice the timing of the change. Make certain that everyone is making the change precisely at the same time. You will notice an immediate expressive effect that is not present when the change is not together.

If the dynamic event is a diminuendo or a crescendo, there is an added difficulty. Your players need to agree on the shape of the change. How fast will the sound get louder or softer? Is it a symmetric shape or does the sound flare at the end of a crescendo? Young players are so eager to please you that they often make all of a crescendo at the beginning and have nothing left for the end. Or they may make an immediate crescendo followed by a decrease in sound, which gives the exact opposite effect of what the composer intended. Where is the loudest point? How loud (or soft) is it?

Try rehearsing these changes outside the context of the music. You can use any warm-up materials or you can extract a few measures from the piece you are learning. Take it slowly and help students understand exactly what you are trying to achieve. Even the youngest of players can be successful if you give them the chance.

Taking the time to teach your students where the dynamics should occur and making sure that everyone agrees on the resulting intensities will give your ensemble a much more expressive and polished sound. ➥

# Personal Growth/Development

*Frank L. Battisti*

*I consider the development of one's potential as a human being a "moral responsibility."*

**INGREDIENTS:**
Love for a subject, and for directors and teachers—a love for music. A passion to learn and grow. A strong work ethic. An open mind.

**SERVES:**
Everyone who loves music and desires to share that love with others.

An individual's growth, development of personal values (TASTE), and concept of quality (AESTHETIC VALUES) are influenced by the contacts they have with people, ideas, and objects throughout life. Formal and informal educational pursuits offer excellent opportunities for personal growth and development. Contact with people, objects, and ideas that are challenging, provocative, and stimulating—ones that provoke questions and do not fit comfortably—offer the best opportunities for personal growth. The evolving, enlightened band director/teacher, emptied of prejudice, makes provisions for continuous contact with exceptional people, objects, and ideas.

Band directors/teachers who pursue personal and professional growth, whose "tanks" are constantly being replenished by contacts with great art, great ideas, and creative people, bring more energy and excitement to their teaching. They enter rehearsal and classrooms excited, anticipating the thrill of being able to share new knowledge, insights, and discoveries with their students.

Leonard Bernstein, in his wonderful book, *The Joy of Music* (1959), describes his passion for conducting and teaching. I make a few substitutions in Bernstein's comment in hopes of making it more relevant to band directors/teachers.

> . . . the conductor [substitute: band director/ teacher] must not only make his orchestra [substitute: band] play, he must make them want to play. He must exalt them, lift them, start their adrenaline pouring, either through cajoling or demanding or raging. But however he does it, he must make the orchestra [substitute: students] love the music as he loves it. It is not so much imposing his will on them like a dictator; it is more like projecting his feelings around

him/her so that they reach the last man/woman in the second violin section [substitute: clarinet or any other section]. And when this happens—when one hundred [substitute: any number you want] men/women [substitute: boys and girls] share their feelings, exactly, simultaneously, responding as one to each rise and fall of the music, to each point of arrival and departure, to each little inner pulse—then there is a human identity of feeling that has no equal elsewhere. It is the closest thing I know to love itself. On this current of love the conductor [substitute: band director/teacher] can communicate at the deepest levels with his players [substitute: students] and ultimately with his audience.

The love of music generated Bernstein's passion for conducting/teaching!

Discovering and pursuing something you love is the key to fulfillment and success in life. Most of us who teach music were motivated to do so by our love of music. It is very important to sustain and strengthen this love by being lifelong students of music. Great teachers are musicians who answer "the call" to share their love of music with others. Conductors/teachers who love music and pursue musical, intellectual, and personal growth will always have much to love and much to share with their students. ➤●

# How to Cook Your Favorite Meals without the Exact Ingredients (Or: Adapting and Adjusting Band Literature for the Unbalanced Ensemble)

*Jay Bocook*

**INGREDIENTS:**
Solid score study, understanding of basic orchestration, creative thinking, and a little bit of "thyme."

**SERVES:**
All composers, students, adjudicators, and audiences alike.

Too often this author has observed concert bands performing music scored for a standard instrumentation, only to see or hear several instruments missing from the group. All of us as band directors have encountered less than perfect instrumentation at one time or another. But to simply ignore the problem and go without particular voices is like cooking and leaving specific ingredients out altogether! By modifying or substituting ingredients (instruments) we find a flavor—a sound—that that better represents the original recipe (score).

Carefully study the recipe (score) . . . don't just start cooking (rehearsing)!

Firstly, find which ingredients, or voices, are missing or need strengthening. Then look at the roles those voices play at any given moment. Ask yourself several questions:

* Is this voice part of the melodic structure, and if so, is the melody strong enough without them?
* Is it part of the harmony here, and do any other instruments have the same chord tone?
* Is the missing voice part of a countermelody and is it doubled anywhere?

Answering these questions will start the conductor on the path towards knowing how and when to make voice substitutions.

Next, find other available ingredients (instrument voices) that substitute well for missing or weak ones, i.e., margarine for butter, or tenor sax for euphonium; crabmeat for lobster or trumpet or clarinet for oboe. Okay, you get the analogies by now. Baritone sax or bass clarinet for tuba. Low clarinets and alto saxes for middle brass. Even marimba or vibes for mid voices. The possibilities are almost endless if you think creatively. Maybe the listener will not be hearing the exact voice, but he/she will be hearing *some* voice. Chords will be complete, countermelodies will be heard, and melody will be secure.

**Problem Solving**

Viewing the score from the composer's/arranger's perspective is the key. For example, in most band scores, grade 4 and below, if there is a third trumpet part, it will rarely be an independent part. It often will be doubling other trumpet parts or other instruments will be doubling it. So, if the ensemble is limited in trumpet players, you can often incorporate three parts into two. Another example: if the trumpets or trombones are playing chords, as in fanfares, and it is written a bit high for the talent level of the group, simply make a downward inversion of the chords. The first trumpet will play what the second has, second plays what the third has, and third plays what the first has, down an octave. One final example here: very technical passages can have selective notes removed to make them more accessible. It is amazing how much better the passage can feel and sound with the omission of very few notes. Just be careful here that the notes that are removed actually make the passage easier. Really understanding instrument fingerings is a big help.

Another common problem in unbalanced instrumentation is that of the bass line. No tubas or low reeds, for example. The truth of the matter is that in band we only have a few instruments that can accomplish the bass line—for example, tuba, baritone sax, bass clarinet, and string bass. If none of these instruments are available, there will simply be no bass sound. This is not a good thing from the composer's point of view. If this situation exists, try substituting an electric bass or a synthesized bass, such as a keyboard. Not ideal, but at least there will be a bass line.

Our final goal is to produce a musical product that keeps the integrity of the original. If done creatively and with complete respect for the composer's intent, we can very effectively adapt and adjust the individual parts to create an opportunity for success. ➤●

# Food for Thought: Does Your Band Sound Better from the Back?

*Peter Loel Boonshaft*

Undoubtedly, any list of truly important ensemble performance concepts will number balance high among them. We all know the importance of good balance to the success of any ensemble. We each attend to balance in our own way, but irrespective of how we teach or practice balance, there may be one "link" missing.

**INGREDIENTS:**
An ensemble trying to achieve better and more consistent balance, set up in a fashion so the conductor can walk around it completely. A composition or warm-up exercise of simple technical demands, so tone and balance are the main performance consideration.

**SERVES:**
Any instrumental or vocal ensemble.

It was 1982. I was three hours into the first rehearsal of guest conducting this wonderful high school band in Oklahoma, and I needed a break. So, I walked to the back of the band room while the host director began rehearsing his band for the portion of the program he was to conduct. The back of the room was lined with large black wooden boxes that were used as packing crate-like cases when the band went on tour. They were arranged like giant Lego® blocks to form a towering, raked wall. I climbed atop those cases, leaned back, and toweled-off while resting. After a few moments of relaxing on this perch, I had a realization. I had just spent the better part of the morning working with this band toward a good sense of ensemble balance. Though I didn't consistently hear that sound while conducting the group, I did hear it beautifully, vividly, now—in the back of the band.

So, I spent some time walking around the band as they performed, listening *not* for whether it was well balanced, but rather for how it sounded from their location in the band. I had always walked around my ensembles, but I was always listening for whether *I* was getting what I wanted, not how *they* heard it from their perspective. Though that may sound like semantic hair-splitting, it has truly made an enormous difference in how I attend to the teaching of ensemble balance.

It was at that very moment I became acutely aware of a problem. From where a tuba player sits in the back of many ensembles, they hear a *very* balanced, possibly ultra-balanced, and blended sound. Taking into consideration the omnidirectional or unidirectional nature of certain instruments, and seating designs that are often used, we ensure a wonderful sound from *that* vantage point: *the back of the band.* Think about it, from that spot: the bass and tenor brass are close by you with a sound that permeates the area like fog, trumpets in front of you "aiming" the sound away, French horn players directing that fantastically rich sound right at you, treble woodwinds a fair distance away with the highest voices farthest away. What do you have? The balanced sound that we strive for everyday. All too often, for many players, the well-balanced sound we describe and define is pretty close to what *they* hear when *we* say the band sounds *poorly* balanced.

Obviously, this is a gross oversimplification. And, though I described this situation using a band as the example (mostly because I liked the quasi-alliteration of the title), it is the same with any ensemble. Of course depth of instrumentation, seating design used, the quality of each performer's tone, characteristics of our rehearsal space, and our own preferences regarding tone and balance will play a large role in this issue, but it does point to a link all too often forgotten. We spend hours working on balance in rehearsals, we study methods and techniques to develop this skill, we invent warm-up exercises to practice a balanced sound, we impart to our players how important a balanced sound is to our success, we play recordings of fine bands, and encourage our students to attend concerts and listen to recordings of professional ensembles.

However, even though we may compare and contrast "balanced" and "unbalanced" sounds in rehearsals, the missing link is that we often do not explain to our players that the sound we strive for is balanced from the front, and that for much of the ensemble this will provide a very unbalanced, or sometimes hyper-balanced, sound to their ears. If left to their own natural, untrained instincts, ensembles will not produce a balanced sound, but is that totally due to lack of effort or understanding, or because from where they sit it sounds pretty good?

Human nature being what it is, why should they work harder if it already sounds good to them? Depending on where they sit, an unbalanced (from the front) sound, can sound just like those recordings of well-balanced ensembles we play for our students. Now, I have always been an advocate of having recordings of remarkable bands playing as students walk in and out of rehearsal, but if left unchecked that may compound the problem. Certainly, we can attempt to fix some problems with changes in seating design, but all too often those changes make another problem worse.

Others far more learned than I have discussed techniques for developing ensemble balance, and my purpose here is not to restate those ideas, but simply to point out one missing part of the equation. Players must understand that what they need to develop and learn is what a balanced ensemble sounds like from *their* seat. In other words: what it must sound like from their vantage point so they can contribute what is necessary for the entire ensemble to sound well-balanced. It is not that we need to strive for a different concept of balance or blend, or teach it differently; it is simply remembering that many of our performers will be listening for a very different quantity and quality of sound than that which we describe as our goal. Once the balance we wish is achieved, we must have our students lock that sound into their memory, as their personal balance goal, even though it may sound unbalanced to them.

The story I referred to happened twenty-three years ago, and though it pointed out to me a very simple notion, I think about it most every rehearsal. Though we all have a different approach to, and ideal of ensemble sound, this simple idea may be helpful. The next time you have a chance, walk to the rear of your ensemble and listen. It is an easy quiz. Just ask yourself if your band sounds better from the back. ➝•

# Guidelines for Choral Music Selection

*Lynn M. Brinckmeyer*

Sometimes new teachers or seasoned teachers new to choral music are at a loss in selecting appropriate octavos for their choral students. Choosing the appropriate literature for your particular ensemble is one of the most important decisions you will make to set up your students for success. In order to select literature that matches your students' skills and potential, you will need to investigate a variety of components in the musical selection.

**INGREDIENTS:**
Choral music. Rubric to assess the following aspects of choral literature.

**SERVES:**
All choral music students.

### Rhythms/Meter
* Are the rhythms easy to count or challenging?
* How much repetition occurs within the rhythmic patterns?
* Does the piece have mixed meters?
* What is the smallest rhythmic subdivision?
* Is the printed score easy to read?
* Are there syncopated rhythms?

### Intervals/Harmonies
* Is the piece in a major or minor key?
* Is it written in a mode or unfamiliar scale?
* Does the selection contain many chromatic alterations?
* How much consonance or dissonance occurs?
* Are the singers expected to sing tritones, unusual chords, clusters?
* Would you consider this an atonal selection?
* What is the largest interval for each voice? the smallest?
* Does the accompaniment assist or challenge the singers?
* Are very young voices expected to sing parallel thirds?
* Is the piece written as partner songs? a canon? with a descant?
* Can novice singers sing the melody successfully while other voices fill out the harmonies?

### Text/Language
* Do the words relate to the singers' world?
* Can they identify with the poetry?

- If in a foreign language, how difficult is it? (Many Latin, Italian, Hebrew, and African songs are easily accessible for young voices.)
- How repetitive is the text?
- Will the students still enjoy singing the text six weeks after they are introduced to the music?
- Is the text sacred or secular?
- Does it have historical significance?
- Is it seasonal or only appropriate for certain religious situations (holiday music, mass, requiem, etc.)?

## Diction/Articulation/Phrasing
- Does the composition require sustained air support?
- How difficult is the phrasing?
- What challenges will the articulation provide?
- Are there voiced consonants?
- How many phrases end with S, R, or L?
- Do accents create a problem?

## Tone
- What tone color is most appropriate for the music?
- How many words contain open/pure vowels?
- Are there numerous French or German vowels?
- Does the piece include troublesome diphthongs?
- Which vowels are more prominent?
- Are the vowels open or closed?

## Dynamics
- Are singers expected to sing very loud for long periods of time?
- Are they required to sing very soft for an extended time period?
- Is it possible to modify to an [a] in the upper ranges and still understand the text?
- Does the composition ask for terraced dynamics or gradual changes in dynamic contrast?
- Sforzando?

## Tempo/Form
- Is the tempo incredibly fast or slow? (Very slow tempos can create challenges for younger voices.)
- Do the tempos change throughout the piece?
- Are there rubato sections? fermatas?
- Is the form strophic? through-composed? song form?
- Are there repeated sections? coda?

## Tessitura/Range
- Are there extremes in vocal ranges for any voice part?
- Are singers expected to sustain high pitches for any length of time?
- Are the lower voices required to sing in the lower ranges consistently?
- How much of the music hangs around the passaggio?
- What key is the piece written in?
- Can your ensemble cover all of the written parts without damaging their voices? (Refrain from having young women sing the tenor part.)
- What key is the piece? (E major, F# major, and G major work well with young voices.)

- Will it accommodate changing voices? (Young men should be able to sing a low D before being considered a true tenor.)
- Is it more appropriate for middle school or high school?

## Audience Appeal
- Does the music support the national music standards/state standards?
- Will the singers enjoy working on and performing the music?
- Will the audience appreciate the performance?
- Does your program follow a particular theme?
- Are the selections chosen to expose students to music of other cultures, music of the masters, etc.?
- Will these music selections add quality to your library?
- Will you want to perform them again in five, ten, or twenty years?

## Accompaniment
- How difficult is the accompaniment?
- Do you have a pianist who can play the accompaniment and all of the parts?
- Are the singers expected to sing with an instrument such as oboe, flute, violin, etc.?

Assessing the music our students sing is as important as assessing their individual skills and musicality. By addressing each of the questions listed here, you will be more equipped to serve the singers in your choirs and create an environment that fosters their growth as musicians. ➞

# Marking the Score for Better Eye Contact

*Michael Burch-Pesses*

Score study is the most important activity of any conductor, and unfortunately it may be the most neglected. Learning the score during rehearsal not only signals a lack of preparedness, but also severely limits the eye contact that is essential to clean and accurate entrances. By combining easy-to-read score markings with increased eye contact during rehearsals, we can rehearse more effectively with better musical results.

**INGREDIENTS:**
Lead pencil, yellow highlighter, red pencil, 30 minutes of quiet time for score study each day, and the commitment to look up from the score, rather than follow every measure with your eyes.

**SERVES:**
All conductors and every musical ensemble.

It may seem difficult at first to set aside quiet time for score study every day, but this commitment will pay big dividends. Try giving up one television show each night, or reduce the time you now spend reading the newspaper. Before long the practice of studying the score will become part of your daily routine, and you will enjoy discovering the "nuggets" in the music.

Begin by identifying the main themes throughout the score and marking the instruments carrying that theme. If the clarinets have the melody, pencil in "CLAR" at that point in the score and highlight it. Do this every time the melody is handed off to a different instrument or section. Make a pencil notation at all tempo changes. An arrow pointing to the left would indicate a ritard, one pointing to the right an accelerando. Highlight these notations so you won't miss them.

Develop your own shorthand to indicate meter changes. I use a triangle to indicate a change to 3/4 time, and a square for a change to 4/4. Other meters might require more inventive symbols, but make them simple and easy to read. Write your chosen symbol at the top of the page where the meter changes occur.

Use the red pencil to fill in crescendos and diminuendos. The more red you see in the score, the more strength should come from the ensemble. Less red means less strength. One of my colleagues uses red in the crescendo as the music gets "hotter," and blue in the decrescendo as the music "cools off." This visual cue is an excellent way to spot a dynamic change without having to squint at the score.

When you have finished marking the score in these four ways, conduct it in your imagination from the beginning. You will see how these markings enable you to cue and to indicate changes in meter, tempo, and dynamics. Use these marks sparingly! Like spices, they can add vibrancy to your recipe or turn it into an unpalatable mess.

The purpose of making these markings is to free you from having to look at the score, so make a commitment to look at the ensemble more than the score. During your first few rehearsals after marking the score according to this recipe, glance at the score only every two measures and otherwise always look at the ensemble. When you do glance down, scan an entire page for your marks so you can anticipate what is coming up. Let the "every two measures" rule simmer until you are comfortable with it. Then expand your eye contact by glancing at the score only every four measures.

The idea is to establish eye contact with your ensemble between glances at the score. Eye contact makes your ensemble feel more secure. Decide that you will make eye contact with every member of your ensemble during every rehearsal. Make it a habit to look at the third clarinets when you cue the clarinet section, not just the firsts or the solo chair. Let every section know you consider them integral to the music by cueing them and looking at them regularly. When your ensemble responds to your gestures, don't forget to smile to reinforce their performance.

When your ensemble members see that you are looking at them as you cue an entrance or change meter, tempo, or dynamic, their performance will improve significantly, and that's when the magic will happen! ➤●

# Effective Ensemble Articulation: Developing Rhythmic Accuracy within the Ensemble

*Charles F. Campbell, Jr.*

When introducing a new composition, conductors are often faced with the task of teaching rhythmic passages that are challenging to the individual performers within the ensemble. I have found that the following approach works well for me.

**INGREDIENTS:**
Chalk, grease board chalk or other markers, and eraser.

**SERVES:**
All ensemble members.

**Step 1:** Prior to the rehearsal, write the rhythmic pattern on the board. This will enable you to explain the rhythm through a visual breakdown.

**Step 2:** Have the students sing the rhythmic pattern on a concert F.

**Step 3:** Ask the students to then play the pattern on a concert F.

**Step 4:** Next play the pattern as it is written on the individual parts—*very slowly*.

**Step 5:** Begin the process of increasing the tempo gradually. Remember keep the tempo at a comfortable pace for the students. As students gain confidence with the tempo, you will be able to increase the tempo to the specifications of the composer.

**Step 6:** Next comes the most difficult part. Students will invariably articulate the parts differently—some too short, others too long. Yes, there will be others who still do not completely understand the rhythmic pattern. At this juncture, I have a principal player perform the pattern until I like the way it sounds. Secondly I ask each individual in the ensemble to emulate this. Identifying those students who can match the principal player enables the conductor to begin the process of playing as an ensemble. Once two can play as one I gradually involve additional players. The conductor will immediately be able to identify those students who need further assistance.

Through isolating the individual players, the conductor is able to teach all those players who understand the rhythmic pattern. These students are now able to play with the exact same style of articulation. Thus, the concept is beginning to approach general understanding.

This step-by-step process will eventually enable every member of the ensemble to play with the accuracy that is expected for the ultimate performance of the composition. ➾

# Educating Future Music Consumers

*John E. Casagrande*

As conductors of school music groups, we have great latitude in selecting the curriculum of our classes: no prescribed textbooks from the central office and no faculty committees to choose what we should use in the classroom. While that freedom allows us to choose the content of our daily lessons, it also carries a huge responsibility to provide our students with the most profound and respected literature of our civilization. Because, the music we choose *is our curriculum*. What we choose to teach our students can influence them as adults, including their future attendance at concerts, choices of recorded music, following music either as a vocation or an avocation, and their level of support for any type of musical activities in their communities.

**INGREDIENTS:**
One dedicated and focused music educator with high standards for great orchestral, vocal, keyboard, and wind music, spanning the past three hundred years. Students that have been well trained in the fundamentals of performance on their respective instruments.

Great, quality music.

**SERVES:**
One to one thousand.

From our first days in a collegiate music education class when we were assigned the task of creating our own philosophy of music education, each of us has struggled to work through the daily trials and tribulations of our profession to keep that philosophy in focus. It is easy to be sidetracked by the strengths and weaknesses of the current crop of students sitting before us in daily rehearsals, the demands of our administrators, our administrative responsibilities, our personal lives, and our musical goals.

Like our peers in those idealistic days of university life, we all wanted to share our love of music and music making with our students. We wanted to expose them to the best music possible and teach them to express themselves through quality literature.

After a few years of teaching, we realize that our students are not all going to become music majors. We must then direct our teaching to the 90 percent who will never be teachers or performers and will become "music consumers."

The goals that should be established (not listed in order of importance) are:

- Train students to become as independent as possible in their musical skills
- Require students to be fully accountable for their performance and actions

- Lead students to experience what a musician must do to prepare for performance
- Educate students to become discriminating musicians and knowledgeable consumers

The first goal—training students to become as independent as possible in their musical skills—involves teaching them to be musically literate: able to recreate a composer's written symbols into musical ideas without telling them "how it goes." Those fundamental skills include learning fingerings, mastering rhythm skills, interpreting what is on the score before them, and developing their proficiency on their instrument to the highest level of which the educator believes they are capable.

The second goal—being fully accountable for their performance and actions—is a life lesson that is an indispensable part of a student's growth, not only as musicians but also as members of society. The rules that are in place in any organization are there for the betterment of the group and must be adhered to. If they are not, there are consequences for those that violate them. Discipline, as well as self-discipline, is a paramount attribute to be learned.

The third goal—experiencing what a musician has to do to prepare for a performance—is probably one of the easier goals to define, yet time-consuming to implement. It simply means that students are accountable to play every note of every piece on a program to the level that we judge them to be capable.

Achieving the third goal is measured by testing students on their parts. This goal goes hand-in-hand with, and is totally dependent upon, their ability to achieve the first goal of being independent musicians.

The fourth and most important goal—educating students to become discriminating musicians and knowledgeable consumers—is based on the director's choice of music and how that music is presented to the students. I have one basic measuring stick to determine the worth of a piece of music: considering that the musical frame of reference for great instrumental music has always been music composed for the symphony orchestra, *could I imagine going to a concert by the Philadelphia Orchestra or the New York Philharmonic and hearing any of those groups play this piece of music?* Difficulty is not a determining factor, but rather, could we imagine a group of professional musicians playing the sounds on that piece of sheet music and making real music?

Through their exposure to and performing the finest quality music within their skill level, students can become discriminating listeners. As intelligent students (as most student musicians are), it doesn't take much lecturing from the podium for students to learn what great music sounds like. And the more quality music they perform, the more discriminating they can become. For students to recognize that a work is a great piece of music is more important than being able to articulate why it is great. If they do go on to become music majors at the collegiate level, they will learn the components of style, harmony, form, and composition that made the music great.

As the group works toward the performance of a composition, small bits of information should be doled out on a daily basis about the composer, style, orchestration, historical style period, form, and other interesting information about the composition itself. Program notes for the concert serve as the body of information about the work, which can also be used for testing.

Following the performance, students should view a video recording of the performance and write critiques of their performance, including comments from their parents about the concert. The critiques become the topic of discussion at the next rehearsal. This exercise enables students to articulate the qualities that they believe produce an artistic performance.

One of the most important decisions a music educator must make is the selection of literature. In training future music consumers, the music educator must begin by selecting literature of the highest quality; it must serve as the model for students entering adulthood. Through exposure to only the finest literature, students' musical tastes can be elevated to a high artistic level.

Music literature *is* our curriculum and we owe it to our students to provide the finest our art has to offer, regardless of their technical level or performance experience. Our selection of literature, representing our own musical tastes, must be shared with our students: the music consumers of the future. ➡●

# A Healthy Serving: Introducing a New Work to Your Ensemble

*Reber Clark*

A method to quickly break a score down into manageable chunks, see their relationship to each other, and to visually present them to one's ensemble, improving mastery of the piece.

**INGREDIENTS:**
One director wanting to improve their ensemble's performance. One score and set of parts.

**SERVES:**
Any ensemble.

Directors come to the initial rehearsal of a work with their score study completed and a good idea of how the piece fits together. The problem is that there are the students to consider. If the performers, especially the inexperienced ones, can "hold the piece in their heads," better and more exciting performances can result. Efficiently presenting to an ensemble how a work fits together is an invaluable tool for the full realization of a piece of music.

This method is based on the four elements of music, in order of importance: rhythm, melody, countermelody, and harmony. In your score, before the initial rehearsal, break the piece by rehearsal numbers into its formal elements, i.e., introduction, major sections, and coda. This is the larger "rhythm" of the work. Circle any transitions, either abrupt or gradual, and label them as such. Identify and circle the occurrences of the main melody or sonic idea and any contrasting melodies or ideas. Ignore any pepperings of motifs here and there; stick to the large meaty chunks. Lastly, consider the harmony *in a general way* in relation to the major sections. Is it major, minor, quartal, quintal, or other? Write these as general indications in the score. Identify climaxes and mark them.

In the initial rehearsal, after the first read-through, have students identify the introduction, major sections, and the coda by rehearsal number. Play these in sections. Draw a very long timeline on the board and provide students with a very general pictorial representation of the piece:

INTRO | Abrupt Transition | A SECTION | Gradual Transition | B SECTION | Abrupt Transition | A SECTION (Repeated) | Gradual Transition | CODA

Of course a theme-and-variations work would appear differently, as would a rondo or other forms. The importance is that no matter what you do, make a simple pictorial representation of the work.

Have students identify the main melody. *Play it.* Write in where the main melody occurs beneath each section on the board. Have students suggest what the countermelody or contrasting idea is. *Play it.* Indicate it on the board. Lastly impart to students a *general* idea of what the harmony does in each section, e.g., major to minor to major. *Play examples.* Indicate it simply on the board. Identify climaxes and *play them.* Indicate where they occur on the diagram.

Playing each section and using a board diagram to indicate each section and its function may seem obvious to the director, but may be revelatory to students. Once a picture of the piece is in the players' heads, common goals will be identifiable. If there is programmatic material attached to the work, impart it. Once climaxes are identified, it is possible to draw a line indicating the "tension and release" of the piece under the timeline. Students can then see why they must remain at pianissimo in certain sections, forte in others, and why crescendos and harmonies are placed the way they are. Students can see where we want to take the audience during the execution of the work and why. It is a rare performance in this medium that is well done without some comprehension on the performers' part as to the flow of the piece.

By performing this exercise in initial rehearsals, the work will come together as a complete piece for each student, rather than a jumble of sensory information with vague climaxes here and there. This engagement of the mind, in addition to the sheer physical execution of the work, can bring real musical meaning to students' awareness. This enhances the ensemble's performance and gives some insight into seemingly abstract structures of works of art.

The unification of mind and body is not to be underestimated! The various relationships between the levels of rhythm, melody, countermelody, and harmony, from the overall rhythm (which is the duration of the piece) to the smallest sixteenth note passing tones in the third clarinet part become apparent the deeper one delves into a work. The relationship of the tension and release line of the work to the shape of the main melodic line might be compared. Ornamentation can be discussed. The director can go as deep as he or she wishes, although a general overview of the piece should be sufficient for most ensembles. Practical experience also indicates that a single consistent diagram on the board is more effective than individual handouts.

This goal of progressively realizing form from chaos applies to innumerable situations in one's life and, for the student who adopts it, will serve to order a larger and more confusing world into more manageable events. ➤●

# Healthy Repertoire for Successful Band Programs

*James Cochran*

Repertoire is the lifeblood of all band programs. Choosing quality repertoire is a very important decision and not to be taken lightly. The musical growth of the entire ensemble depends on it. Many directors choose their repertoire by making choices from only listening to an excerpt of a work on a demo CD or by playing a new piece from a composer that has "worked" for them in the past, which is music too often filled with formulaic writing and tired clichés. Our students deserve our best effort in choosing quality music. Here are some vital ingredients to consider when making these important choices.

**INGREDIENTS:**
Form and structure that is coherent, balanced, and distinctive. Variety in texture and timbre. Transparency. Musical depth. Emotional expressiveness.

**SERVES:**
The entire ensemble.

One of the best repertoire resources for the band director is a series of books entitled *Teaching Music through Performance in Band*, published by GIA. I often recommend a work found in volume 3, entitled *Resting in the Peace of His Hands*, by John Gibson. This work was written in 1994 for Jack Delaney and the Southern Methodist University Meadows School of the Arts Wind Ensemble. It was inspired by a relief sculpture by Kaethe Kollwitz (1867–1945), which the composer encountered while visiting the Busch-Reisinger Museum at Harvard University. Mr. Gibson knew nothing of the artist, nothing of the origin of the work, and nothing of the origin of the title at the time he encountered the sculpture. He states, "the work expressed to me a remarkable sense of peace and that I would never lose the impression it made upon me." Mr. Gibson writes further that the sculpture was a very personal work, intended to express "the feeling of utter peace," contrary to the major body of her work, intended to express utter torment.

When we analyze the work, we see it contains all the ingredients listed above. The piece is cast in ABA form with a short coda. It is a common form for much of the wind band repertoire, however, upon closer examination, we discover that the return of the A section is not an exact repetition of the original material. In fact, there is considerable variety in timbre and texture in this section and throughout the work. Transparency permeates the entire piece as the only tutti scoring occurs in the brief B section. The fourth and fifth ingredients, musical depth and emotional expressiveness, are created, explored, and intertwined, as the composer expresses the struggle between utter torment and utter peace by presenting dissonantly tinged melodies and harmonies that resolve in the poignant duet at measure 106 and build to the wonderfully triumphant conclusion.

The duties and responsibilities of the band director in the twenty-first century are multitudinous, and many of them have little to do with the musical growth of the ensemble. This very important task of choosing quality repertoire should be paramount on the conductor's to-do list. Performing repertoire of the highest stature and quality will produce substantial and long-lasting rewards. ➞●

# Teaching Creativity through the Use of Graphic Notation

*Michael Colgrass*

In our system of music education, children learn to play an instrument through conventional notation, which makes them very self-conscious about mistakes. In graphic notation, there are no mistakes—only gestures. But after being trained on major and minor scales, graphics sound unusual to kids at first. They need a little time to get used to making these sounds in a new way, because they are, in effect, improvising.

**INGREDIENTS:**
The ingredients in this recipe help students learn how to:

* Invent their own systems of music making
* Play their instruments without fear of making "mistakes," since there are no "right or wrong" notes in graphics
* Create music and understand the overall musical creative process
* Read conventional written music with a new perspective, understanding the reasons behind notation
* Improvise on their instruments
* Gain greater control of their instruments
* Sing, and see the benefits of singing the music they play
* Develop leadership and communication skills

**SERVES:**
All students and teachers interested in a creative approach to music making.

**Appetizer**
1. Ask students to think of a sound, then to imagine a mark they might make on a blackboard to represent that sound. Explain that the empty space on a plain blackboard (no ledger lines) is a potential soundscape for the voice—with the top of the board representing the highest the voice can go and the bottom, the lowest.
2. Make a mark on the blackboard and ask the kids to sing it.
3. Hand chalk to one of the kids and ask him/her to make a second mark, then sing it, then to hand the chalk to someone else.
4. Continue until a soundscape has been created.

5.  Ask the group for suggestions on how they could sing the soundscape together. When someone starts to give an idea, ask him or her to come up to the blackboard and lead a performance. Perform the piece several times, with different students leading.
6.  Explain that they just recreated the past one thousand years of music development—inventing sounds, creating a notation, inventing the conductor, and performing the piece.

ASSIGNMENT: Everybody come in with a graphic piece for the next session. At this session, each student draws his/her piece on the blackboard and leads the group through a performance of it.

## Salad
1.  Form a group of students who want to create graphic pieces, calling them the "composition team." This team gets together with the teacher and creates many pieces, individually and in tandem, as desired, creating new graphic symbols to suit the sounds they invent.
2.  Hand out copies of the Graphic Notation Chart to band members and drill the examples explaining each as you go.

ASSIGNMENT: Practice these graphic symbols on your instrument at home, and be prepared to be tested on them.

## Main Dish
*Preparation of Band Members to Play Graphic Pieces*
To prepare children to play graphic pieces with confidence and skill, they need to practice playing their instruments reading graphic notation. On page 28 is a set of four basic forms of graphic notation that the composition team could use. The band director practices these forms with the band, explaining exactly what the kids should do, as necessary. He or she may also give private instruction to individuals. Then all students are tested individually on all twelve forms, with coaching given where needed.

> NOTE: The band members developing skill and confidence in the playing of these twelve basic graphic forms is the key to getting a smooth performance of the composition teams' graphic pieces, in the same way that practicing scales and chords is the way to prepare a band to play conventionally notated music.

## Dessert
1.  The composition team brings in finished graphic compositions and leads the band through performances of them.
2.  Continue this process over a period of weeks until the composers and the players become skilled at graphics and are used to performing them without inhibition.
3.  The teacher can then explain how the graphics correspond to actual music notation, i.e., staccato and legato, crescendo, sforzando, forte piano, glissando, accents, accelerando and ritardando, trills, breath accents, etc.

**Examples of graphic notation—also create your own.**

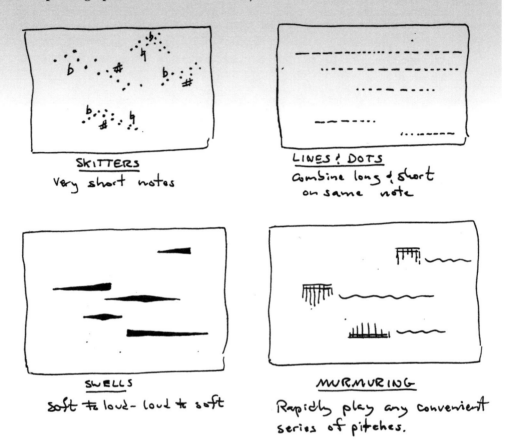

SKITTERS
Very short notes

LINES & DOTS
Combine long & short on same note

SWELLS
soft to loud - loud to soft

MURMURING
Rapidly play any convenient series of pitches.

# Linear Balance

*Gary Corcoran*

The term *balance* can be confusing to young conductors because it has different meanings in different contexts. Understanding the concepts behind it is crucial to effective conducting and teaching, as well as to meaningful performances.

**INGREDIENTS:**
A well-prepared and well-marked score that will serve to clearly illustrate the four musical materials described below. Have each "priority group" play separately, so others can pay attention without having to play, and then start adding groups one by one beginning with the "Sustained Harmonic Material." Be sure to include the appropriate percussion parts as you designate priority groups.

**SERVES:**
All instrumental students, composers, audiences.

In some contexts, *balance*, like the term *blend*, can be described by a literal translation of the word *unison*: one sound. It can also be used to refer to a state of harmonic weighting, in which chord members are emphasized equally or adjusted to produce a specific effect. A balanced instrumentation means that instruments are combined proportionately to produce characteristic wind ensemble sonority. To achieve correct balance, the conductor must juxtapose the various shadings of foreground and background lines so that the listener can clearly perceive all the layers of music.

While studying the score, decide how the music must sound to you and what steps you must take to balance musical lines. Examine each phrase to consider how the various parts should be weighted in relation to each other. Each "subsection" of the ensemble (e.g., 1st trumpet, 2nd trumpet, or 3rd trumpet) must have a balanced volume and "unison" sound so that individual tone qualities do not protrude. If musical lines are doubled, the desirable sonority and volume level will depend on the nature of the composition, the context of the passage, and the conductor's own instincts.

Although saying that "the trombones are too loud at letter D" may get the job done for now, students should develop an understanding of how their parts fit into the whole picture as the composition progresses. Fine musicians learn to sense when it is important to play out and when they must back off. Young players who have not yet developed such skills will require some explicit assistance.

Most composers write uniform dynamic markings in all parts and rely upon the conductor and performers to properly adjust the balance. Others indicate foreground and background by including contrasting dynamic levels for various sections of the ensemble, usually limiting the distinction to melody and accompaniment. The conductor should be attentive to this factor, whether or not the composer establishes balance.

Inexperienced players are likely to gravitate toward the dynamic level they perceive to be common within the whole group. (I refer to this type of sound as *bandissimo*.) Make your students aware that dynamic markings are relative, not absolute, and that they will have to make adjustments to suit the expressive intent of the passage, the thickness of the scoring (including the amount and nature of the doubling), the interrelationship of musical lines, and the period in which the music was composed.

Players should determine the relative importance of their parts based on both what they see on the page and what they hear being played by other sections of the band. Conductors can help them do this by setting some priorities:

1.  **MELODIC MATERIAL.** This is the "melody" or "primary material," as played by any number of instruments. It may also include a harmonization of the melody that moves simultaneously with the melody in identical, or similar, rhythm.
2.  **COUNTERMELODIC MATERIAL.** Continuous countermelodies or occasional countermelodic fragments should be heard clearly but in most cases, should remain secondary to the melody.
3.  **RHYTHMIC HARMONIC MATERIAL.** This background material has the dual function of providing a rhythmic setting that emphasizes or contrasts melodic and countermelodic material, while also providing harmonic support. It usually helps to establish the "style" of the music at this point.
4.  **SUSTAINED HARMONIC MATERIAL.** These are the longer note values that have prompted many a frustrated director to quip, "If all you have are whole notes, you can assume that you are not playing the melody!" Sustained harmonic voices are important, but they should usually yield in volume to moving parts.

Although the elements mentioned above might not all be present at any given point in the music or in all styles of music, the relationships of the existing parts will remain the same.

The relative strength of percussion parts may be weighed according to the contribution of each part. For example, the mallet instruments may double melodic material while the snare drum, timpani, and other accessories reinforce rhythmic harmonic material, and the bass drum accentuates the sustained harmonic material. When the percussion section is playing alone, priority is usually granted to the pitched instruments.

Balance priorities often shift suddenly. Those sections playing sustained harmonic parts may suddenly have an important countermelodic fragment when the melody comes to rest on a sustained note. During an introduction or a transitionary passage, the rhythmic harmonic material may assume a primary role until the melody enters. In polyphonic music, entrances of the subject take priority over the existing counterpoint.

Sometimes conductors will realign balance for a specific effect. In marches, for example, the conductor may choose to highlight an appealing countermelody rather than to play a strict repetition of a particular strain. If carefully handled, adjustments in balance can produce exciting results.

In almost any group some thinning or doubling of parts may be needed at times to compensate for those sections of the band that are not as strong as others, or for problems in the original scoring. Cross-cued scores are one solution for a conductor of a band with incomplete instrumentation. Otherwise, the conductor must use whatever means are at his disposal to assure that each musical element is adequately audible in the band's performance. Teach your players to learn to identify the nature of their role at any given point. A considerable amount of rehearsal time can be saved if the students themselves consciously adjust their dynamic level. It may be helpful for them to write "(1)," "(2)," "(3)," or "(4)," (corresponding to the list of priorities above) on their parts, in passages where balance problems persist or where their relative importance suddenly changes.

As with other elements of music performance, balance is affected by context, stylistic practices, the strengths and weaknesses of the ensemble, and the conductor's individual taste. Establishing specific priorities for balance is a starting point to help your band to render an effective and aesthetically pleasing performance. ➥

# Creating Better Balance and Raising Student Awareness of Parts Other than Their Own

*Paula A. Crider*

Band students tend to focus on that which is of most immediate concern, e.g., their individual part, closing their ears to anything else occurring around them. The following "recipe" is designed to provide a creative and fun method by which to make students more aware of the function of other musical lines, and how individual parts fit into the musical whole. The primary function of this exercise is to provide a means by which student listening skills may be encouraged to grow and to extend in new directions. It also provides a refreshing change of rehearsal pace.

**INGREDIENTS:**
1 medium band director, moderately seasoned
2 cups imagination (or more to taste)
1 bottle fine wine (consumed the evening prior while cooking up lesson plans)
1 familiar piece of music, preferably a march, but not coarsely chopped
178 lb. thoroughly stewed administrator (may be omitted)
1 fresh band thoroughly scrubbed and washed
1 very liberal serving of discipline
2 lb. patience while ingredients are mixed
Scramble thoroughly.

**SERVES:**
Large ensembles as well as smaller, more intimate gatherings.

1.  Select a piece of music with which the band is familiar, and that the ensemble is able to perform with a high level of success. For the initial presentation, a march works quite well. Each player must have his/her own piece of music.
2.  Instruct the members of the ensemble to change chairs, keeping in mind the following rules:

    • Band members may sit anywhere within the rehearsal setup, but may not sit next to someone playing the same part.
    • Where possible, band members should seat themselves next to (or in between) instruments different than their own.

Once ensemble is rearranged—and be patient, the novelty will create some spirited discussion—conduct a first playing through the entire piece. Any cues given by the conductor constitute a great directional challenge!

After the first play-through, seek student feedback by asking such questions as:

- Did you hear a part that you haven't heard before?
- How does your part fit/relate to the sounds of the players to your right and/or left?
- What did you learn from this experience?

Once the initial play-through has occurred, the director may begin to direct students to listen for and identify various voice parts, counter melodic lines, harmonic rhythm, etc.

Benefits of this exercise include:

- Heightened awareness of musical lines other than those of the individual performer.
- A perceived need on the part of the student to perform his part with greater accuracy because he or she is playing next to a new set of ears.
- Taking students out of the "comfort zone" of playing alongside like instrument parts. Promotes greater individual responsibility.
- Provides creative variety in rehearsal.

Ultimately, this procedure may be performed with more challenging music. As with a four-star meal, if carefully prepared, this recipe never fails to provide a memorable and enriching experience. ➤●

# The "Z" Dimension in Performance: Building Individual Awareness of Place within the Whole

*Thomas C. Duffy*

Performing musicians focus greatly on moving through time and the harmonic relationship of their part to all the others. On a graph, the X axis (horizontal) might reflect the units of time, either as beats or subdivisions of beats. The Y axis (vertical) might reflect the harmony structure, which may change from point to point on the X axis. The Z axis, which invokes the concept of linear algebra (a third dimension, if you will), may reflect the placement of an individual part in the overall timbre soundscape.

**INGREDIENTS:**
Musicians with pencils and ears. Music that has melody lines scored across several different instrumental families.

**SERVES:**
The composer, conductors, and musicians, and ultimately the audience!

How often do performers have no idea of the relative potential of dynamics and tone color? These musicians may overplay or underplay their parts, citing defensively, "But it says mezzo forte!" Or, "Of course you can't hear me; it says mezzo piano and I'm muted!" They may not understand that certain musical instructions are not absolute but, rather, relative.

This is a conditioned response. If players were more aware of how their individual sounds contribute to the overall music, they would have a chance of taking responsibility for the consistent and deliberate realization of their parts.

Let's make a distinction between rhythmic accuracy and intonation, and timbral and tonal balance. Progress through time is associated with the X axis of a graph. Placement within a vertical harmony as one moves through time is associated with the Y axis of a graph. The Z dimension addresses the relationship between an individual part and the whole, in the areas of dynamics and timbre.

Here is an exercise for both conductors and players. Take a piece of music that has a melody line scored across several instrumental families. Let's use *Lincolnshire Posy*, movement I, as an example. Practice the first movement until the band plays it with rhythmic accuracy, moving together, acknowledging the unit pulse even in the multi-voice section from measure 18 to measure 34. Go back to the first section (mm. 1–17). Ask only the harmonized melody to play (bassoons, horns, and trumpets). Decide or, as an exercise, ask your students to consider, which voice of the harmonized melody is the principal voice, and which are harmonizations. (The *vox principalis* is played by the horns and bassoons.) Have the bassoons and horns play.

The conductor should have an idea of how the melody should sound. I prefer a melodic timbre in which the double reed sound predominates. This is very easily accomplished, given that the horns are stopped and could allow the reed sound to prevail. (The bassoons and horns then would mark their parts "+bsn.") However, it would be equally viable to ask the bassoons to play so that the stopped horn sound is predominant (marked as "+hn."), or so that both timbres are equally represented ("=hn" and "=bsn." The equal representation is not unlike the organ *diapason* stop). This kind of experimentation is comparable to adjusting the tone controls on a sound system, boosting or lessening the bass, midrange and treble.

Having arrived at a workable formula for the *vox principalis,* add the harmony trumpet parts to the bassoon/horn melody. The tasks for the bassoons and horns are to listen for each other and maintain the agreed-upon timbral relationship (the Z domain), while maintaining accurate rhythmic (X domain) and intonation technique (Y domain). When asked at any given point, "Who are your Z-partners?" horns and bassoons should be able to identify each other.

Trumpets that accompany the melody in this section are also Z-partners of the melody, and should have an idea of how their parts relate to the *vox principalis*. Players should mark their parts to help them remember who it is they should be listening for. (Trumpets might mark their parts "=hn.+bsn.," which means that they should match the horns' dynamic, while allowing the bassoon sound to predominate.) Finding one's Z-partner is an increasingly difficult task as the music becomes more dense or more polyphonic.

A conductor can create different soundscapes by adjusting the relationships between Z-partners when instruments of different timbres are given a single or harmonized melody line.

Try this exercise with other pieces of music.

Percy Aldridge Grainger: *Handel in the Strand*, beginning to letter A. Set up a timbral soundscape between Z-partner instruments that share the opening eighth-note figures: Voice 1 = Trumpets, xylophone, and E-flat, solo, and 1st clarinet (*vox principalis*); Voice 2 = 2nd clarinets and euphonium; Voice 3 = alto clarinet, bassoons, string bass; Voice 4 = 3rd clarinets/bass clarinet.

Peter Mennin: *Canzona*, letter B–C. Set up a soundscape between Z-partner instruments that are scored with the melody: piccolo, flutes, oboes, E-flat clarinet, B-flat clarinets, and cornet 1. (What tone color should predominate? Try different combinations.) Ten measures after B: set up a soundscape between Z-partner instruments in the bass melody: bass clarinet, bassoon, euphonium, basses, and string bass.

If your performers accurately record the instructions that generate certain soundscapes, they will be able to more consistently realize the music as sculpted by the conductor.

The conductor must then decide when the composer has notated the music so as to preclude tonal experimentation, or when it is appropriate to "adjust the tone control on the big band radio!"

# Structuring Taped Assignments for Maximum Learning

*Cheryl Floyd*

So you want them to practice, do you? Just like the old saying, if you want then to watch, give them something to look at. And if you want them to practice, give them an assignment with music of substance!

**INGREDIENTS:**
Cassette player. Metronome. Method book. Assignment sheet.

**SERVES:**
Instrumental groups of all ages.

Have you ever noticed how excited students are when you pass out a new piece of music? Motivation is high, questions are asked, and all instruments go home. Do you ever wonder how to sustain that interest? Consider giving them something motivating and pertinent to practice! Try what I call practice tapes.

I have found that students especially enjoy making practice tapes, because it empowers them to give me their best product. There is no limit to the number of times a student can record and rerecord their assignment. They alone make the judgment as to when it represents their best efforts. And, remember every "take" equates to more home practice . . . sneaky, huh?

The grading of these tapes also creates a less stressful situation for me. I can critique the recordings during my planning period, at home at my leisure, or virtually anywhere I have a few minutes and a cassette player at hand. No class or group instructional time is lost. The feedback is instantaneous, as I verbalize my comments, evaluation, and grade on the same tape, and return it to the student. The student can then rehear their performance and immediately listen to my recorded suggestions for improvement. Students love the instant, personal feedback and their parents welcome the opportunity to listen and be "in the loop" regarding their student's musical achievement. Progress is accelerated and communication with the parents is ongoing.

To track each student's development I also keep a log of my comments. I have learned that this documentation helps me monitor each student's ongoing progress. Yes, it does take a little extra effort but the investment of time is well worth it when I find it necessary to give an overall assessment of a student's strengths and weaknesses or document an assigned grade.

As I structure each grading period's assignment I am mindful of several factors. I always strive to identify and clearly articulate performance goals for both individual students and the class as a whole. Scale, thirds, arpeggios, and technical drills such as the Clark studies are always a part of the assignment. Music being prepared for honor band auditions is sometimes included. Every assignment is intended to develop a specific aspect of the student's skills.

Many times the audition material for honor band or all district band tryouts can be quite intimidating for young players. In order to facilitate learning and encourage participation of less experienced students, assign part of the assignment for one tape and the rest for the next one. More advanced (or motivated) students might receive bonus points for preparing the entire selection.

Duets and small ensembles are also utilized. Some assignments are intended to be prepared, recorded, and performed by two or more students. In so doing, students learn to work together, heighten listening skills, and develop ensemble awareness. Simply working on a task and achieving a common music goal is a beneficial enterprise for all students. Students enjoy pacing one another as they work together to complete the assignment.

For convenience, I prefer to use a class method book and scale sheets for most of the assignments. However, I often use individual method books or musical excerpts as special exercises or bonus assignments.

A metronome is "standard equipment" for all students and must be used during the recording sessions. A tempo range (highest to lowest acceptable tempo) is announced for all assignments. They are referred to as "tempo windows." Within these tempo ranges students can set their own goal, depending on the skill level they hope to attain. This component of the project helps give students "ownership" of the ongoing quest for practice and improvement. Advanced students enjoy the challenge of the more demanding metronome setting, and the young students can still have a sense of accomplishment at the slower tempos.

Students are not left unguided. All material is covered in class and/or in sectionals, and students are encouraged to make a first recording immediately after each assignment is covered in class. Thus they have a reference point as they proceed.

Consider having a few extra credit card–sized metronomes on hand. They are available at a nominal cost. The same might be true regarding inexpensive hand-held cassette recorders, however, you will probably quickly discover that most students have their own.

Many students love bonus opportunities. For example, give a bonus for students who turn in their recording early. If a specified week has been set as a deadline for a particular assignment, consider giving ten bonus points for students who turn in work on Monday. Hearing a recording turned in early affords me the opportunity to make sure that the assignment is clear and that students are on task. Conversely, a penalty can be accessed for students who fail to turn in their tape by the end of the week.

A bonus can also be awarded for students who wish to perform extra assignments, such as playing scales, thirds, or arpeggios for two or more octaves. Thus students are encouraged to become familiar with the entire range of their instruments. The options are limitless.

The utilization of practice tapes is a valuable motivational and diagnostic tool for students of all ages and levels of achievement. They create the prospect for personalized interaction (think: mini-private lesson) with all students. In turn, each individual student is afforded the opportunity to acquire a sense of confidence and self-esteem as they define their performance goals and personal levels of achievement. Who could ask for more? ➡

# For Wholesome Nutrition, the Music Matters

*Richard Floyd*

While any music will serve the purpose of developing fundamentals such as tone quality, technique, rhythm, and other ensemble skills, only the finest compositions will lead students to an understanding and deeper appreciation of music as the art form it is. Quality repertoire should be the cornerstone of any music program.

### INGREDIENTS:

A blend of exemplarily music selections carefully selected to accommodate yet challenge the technical and intellectual abilities of student musicians. Use only premium-grade ingredients.

### SERVES:

All students who seek meaningful and inspirational music experiences.

Schumann said, "No children can be brought to healthy manhood on candy and pastry." Who would disagree? After all, our society is barraged with a steady stream of data proclaiming the necessity of a nutritious diet to ensure physical wellbeing and healthy growth. Parents are steadfast in their desire to see that their children "eat right." School lunch programs go to great pains to foster good eating habits and cultivate a healthful dining regimen for students. There is unity in the notion that young people should be properly nourished.

Our culture has similar expectations in most academic disciplines. English, math, and science teachers have extensive curriculum guides and textbooks that define the scope and depth of information that will be explored in their disciplines. Here, too, their "diet" is set.

Now is there a corollary in what we "serve up" on the musical menu we prepare for our music students? Schumann apparently thought so, since he went on to say, "Musical like bodily nourishment must be solid." A trip to the dictionary reveals that the word "solid" is defined as being built out of strong substantial materials and providing ample nourishment. How does that definition measure up when we apply it to the countless repertoire decisions that we as band directors make each year?

Let's face it. We have a unique and sometimes overwhelming responsibility. To a great degree we determine the text and subject matter that we will explore in each of our performance-based music classes. The goals and aspirations we hold as conductor and teacher will define the quantity and quality of "nourishment" we provide for our students. At the same time the music we select also makes a significant statement about the musical values to which we aspire and the "musical health" we wish to impart.

Certainly there are many influences that affect our choices. Festival preparation, musical growth, technical limitations, student motivation and, yes, entertainment are all factors that enter into the selection process. The list of rationale can be endless. However, under all circumstances perhaps the key word should be "balance." Just as a balanced diet is essential for physical health, a balance of musical priorities is necessary for musical, technical, and artistic growth. And, yes, the source of the "nourishment" should be of the highest quality available.

So what constitutes a balanced musical diet? At the supermarket, one is confronted with countless choices. Dining out affords us limitless options, from national "fast food" chains to the most exquisite of dining experiences. A visit to our local music dealer or the exhibit hall at any music conference affords us a similar range of options. A significant portion of the music on the shelves will be designed to entertain, to replicate last year's "hit," or conform to a very predictable formula of compositional craft. But the inventory will also include a growing collection of "band, orchestra, or vocal classics" plus works by major composers, compositions that offer the potential for exceptional musical growth and repertoire that represents hundreds of years of cultural heritage. The music we put in our "shopping basket" will determine our educational menu and ultimately the musical health of our students.

Repertoire selection must be measured against criteria that lead us to worthy musical choices. Which is better? A catchy tune supported by an endless ostinato or an artistically scored folk song that represents the musical heritage of mankind? Will a student's musical growth be best served by happily performing a clever melody over a redundant chord progression, or the study of a finely crafted work that meets the highest criteria for our repertoire?

Likewise, looking at cartoons does not create an awareness of the beauty in great paintings. Reviewing pop culture does not afford us insights into the greatness of mankind. Reading comics is not a threshold to literary masterworks. Thus it stands to reason that we cannot build an appreciation for great music and instill the joy of performing significant musical works with a product of lesser quality.

The challenge then becomes one of always seeking the finest music available at your performance level. Be vigilant in your quest for only the best and most nutritious music for your students. At any given time, make sure that there is a variety of music being explored, including compositions from a variety of musical periods and styles. Have at least one work in the folder that is by or references a composer found in *Grove Dictionary of Music and Musicians*. Embrace music that offers opportunities for musical independence rather than music that is liberally cross-scored to simply make an ensemble "sound good." Finally, choose a balanced diet of music that is going to broaden rather than limit each student's musical horizons.

There is another deciding factor that must be central to the goal of "dishing up" wholesome musical nourishment. Dale Clevenger said that music should be "90 percent art and only 10 percent craft." Yet students love technical challenges and the energy level present in music that might be best defined as "finger aerobics." Certainly we must expand our student's performance skills. That is a given. Appropriate technical and rhythmic challenges are certainly essential "dietary needs." However, it is incumbent that we choose some music that abandons the quest for enhanced dexterity and rather exists solely to "touch the heart." Such music is intended to be expressive rather than impressive. This is music that frees the students' minds and souls from technical issues and allows them to explore the expressiveness that is inherent in this musical genre. A simple setting of last year's hit ballad or holiday favorite will not suffice. What we must seek is music that is artistically crafted and intellectually challenging. Choose wisely.

There is a final caveat. It is no secret that children, if left to their own devices, will eat what they like. They will always gravitate to and devour what is familiar, regardless of dietary needs. Musical tastes are no different. Students like and want more of what they understand. Consequently, it is our responsibility to challenge their musical tastes, expand their artistic horizons, and give them musical fare that is nourishing, wholesome, and lasting.

You must plan your menu with care and concern for your student's musical sustenance. You are the chef. *Bon appetit!* ➤

# Involving Teachers in the School Band Program: A Recipe for Success

*Eileen Fraedrich*

The attitude of the classroom teacher toward band is crucial to the success of the school band program. How can the director ensure that the teacher's attitude is a positive one? Following is a recipe for fostering a cooperative school climate, resulting in increased student participation.

**INGREDIENTS:**
Enthusiastic classroom teachers. An upcoming performance. Access to instruments.

**SERVES:**
All school band programs, but especially elementary pull-out band programs.

A necessary component of an excellent band program is student involvement. A strong, vital program attracts and retains students. Many factors influence the participation rate of students—the director's recruitment efforts, the reputation of the band program, economic factors, the presence of other programs in the school which draw from the same student body, and the attitude of the classroom teachers toward the band program, to name a few. This last factor, the attitude of the classroom teacher toward the band program, cannot be overlooked, as this can make or break a band. For that reason, it is incumbent upon the director to ensure that classroom teachers have a positive perception of the band. Involving the teachers in the band program is one way to gain their support. Following is an idea that I have used in three of my schools with much success, and the rewards in terms of the band program have been significant.

Before an upcoming performance, poll the faculty to see how many teachers played band instruments as students. (This is easily done via e-mail. At each of my schools, quite a few teachers had played instruments.) Invite those teachers to join the band for a performance. Most will probably be understandably hesitant at first, as they will not have played in some time, but stress that they will be given folders with fingering charts, that they may play on any or all pieces, that you will try to borrow instruments for them to use, if necessary, and that you will be available to help them. In a school of average size, I would expect at least a handful of teachers to respond. Invite those teachers to attend a student rehearsal, if it can be worked into their schedules, as well as an optional rehearsal or two for teachers only.

Give some thought to the seating of teachers at rehearsals and at the performance—whenever possible, try to group them together for moral support. At the performance, be sure to publicly recognize those teachers who participate—perhaps have corsages or some other token of thanks for them. (I put a Hershey's "Symphony Bar" on each teacher's chair.) The enthusiasm of the students and teachers involved in this joint effort can be contagious, with more teachers likely to come forth to participate on subsequent concerts.

What are the benefits of involving teachers in this way? Firstly, the teachers can be very good players who are a real asset to the band (some of mine played trombone, horn, clarinet, flute, percussion, and even tuba), but more importantly, the students in the band, playing alongside their teachers, see that playing an instrument is an interest that they can pursue throughout their lives—it's a multigenerational activity that brings joy and fulfillment to people of all ability levels. Teachers and students are equals in this endeavor, working toward a common goal, and this fosters a tremendous feeling of school unity and camaraderie that can be difficult to achieve by other means.

Students respect and want to emulate their teachers—the students in the audience, seeing their own teachers and classmates performing together, are more likely to participate in the following year. A personal benefit for the director is the pleasure of interacting with other teachers—an element often lacking in the daily routine of an elementary itinerant teacher. Finally, the classroom teachers, having been involved, can better appreciate what it takes to make a good band program. When the director needs to pull the students for an extra rehearsal or runs overtime with a class, the classroom teacher who has played in the band can understand why this happens and is apt to be more forgiving.

What about those teachers who don't play instruments? Is it possible to involve them in the program? Absolutely. There are certain band pieces that call for narration or include a skit. One such piece is *Aunt Rhodie's Appetite* by Joseph Compello (Carl Fischer). This is a fun piece, suitable for elementary school beginners on a first concert. It is made up of ten easy tunes, many of which appear in beginning band method books, tied together with a humorous skit, which can involve the principal or classroom teachers as actors. Try inviting a teacher to guest-conduct a piece or to help out in the percussion section and the same aforementioned benefits will apply. You might even inspire a teacher to begin learning a band instrument. At one of my schools, I taught a beginning band class for teachers. It met before school, once a week, and had almost twenty participants!

By including faculty and staff members in the band experience, both personal and professional rewards can result. The rewards of friendships forged with colleagues, a stronger band program, and increased student participation are well worth the effort involved.

# Serve It Fresh!

*Rob Franzblau*

All chefs understand the importance of serving their creations at the moment when they're done. A fallen soufflé just can't compare to a perfectly timed one, even though all the ingredients might be the same. As teachers, we also want our rehearsals to sparkle with that same feeling that comes when we connect with our students in an animated, fresh atmosphere. Here are three tips to help any recipe in this cookbook retain its "fresh-out-of-the-oven" feeling when served at your rehearsal table.

**INGREDIENTS:**
Whatever you have cooked up for your ensemble, sprinkle it liberally with genuine enthusiasm, zoom in/zoom out, and fast pacing before serving.

**SERVES:**
The entire group. The positive vibes from these freshness tips are contagious!

**FRESHNESS TIP 1. Genuine Enthusiasm**
When your tone of voice, eye contact, pace, facial expression, and sense of humor all contribute to an impression that there's nothing else you would rather be doing right now—when you're totally "in the moment"—you're showing genuine enthusiasm. Feeling it isn't enough; your students need to see it shining through you! Nobody wants to follow a leader who isn't truly excited about where he or she is going, so let it show! Confusion, anxiety, insecurity, worry, and lack of energy will block all attempts at showing genuine enthusiasm and are often the result of poor planning, so study your scores and plan your rehearsals with care. Then, if you're truly excited by what you're teaching, make an effort to show it in your voice (modulating pitch and volume), eye contact (make it frequently), pace (keep it fast), and facial expression (smile!).

*Warning:* Another consequence of poor planning is overcompensating with *insincere* enthusiasm—we've all seen examples of the over-the-top conductor/cheerleader on steroids. Teenagers (rightfully) have little tolerance for this poor substitute and will tire of it quickly.

**FRESHNESS TIP 2. Zoom In, Zoom Out**
By starting to rehearse large "chunks" of music (entire movements, sections, or phrases) and gradually zooming in on specific technical problems in specific instruments, we help our students to see the problem as theirs, to own the problem, and to take responsibility for the solution. However, only by then putting the small pieces gradually back together again, by

zooming back out to play larger sections of music, can technical development be put to a musical purpose.

We all know that correct notes and rhythms are just a means to an end, and that musical expression is all about telling a story to the listener. Music acquires meaning only in how individual notes, phrases, and sections relate to each other, how they repeat, contrast, anticipate, and develop. However, when we disconnect the notes from the story in grueling drill sessions without putting the notes back in context of larger musical phrases, it becomes almost impossible for our students to reconnect to the story and care about the music. Zoom in and out throughout your rehearsal to keep the message meaningful and fresh!

### FRESHNESS TIP 3. Fast Pacing

Think of pacing as the time that elapses between the end of one activity (anything in which the student is actively participating) and the beginning of another. The shorter the average time, the faster the pace is. For the student, the activity may certainly be playing their instrument, but it also may include singing, counting rhythms, marking their parts with a pencil, clapping a steady beat, focused listening while another section plays, answering a question based on their listening, offering an opinion, or taking notes from a brief talk about the composer.

The trick of moving rehearsals at a fast pace is to eliminate the downtime between these activities, and to flow from one to the next *with as little talking by the conductor as possible*. Try the "five-second rule" on yourself: if you can stop the ensemble, give some specific feedback, set a performance goal for the next activity, and start the group again all in five seconds, you're doing really well.

Students are no different than you or me—we learn best by doing, rather than being told. If you want to keep it fresh, keep your words to a minimum and keep the activities flowing. ➤●

# Balanced Percussion Education (Or: Bored Percussionists: A Recipe for Disaster)

*David C. Fullmer*

Percussionist boredom can be avoided by trying this step-by-step recipe for a delicious, nutritious, and well-balanced percussion class curriculum your kids will love.

**INGREDIENTS:**
Sixteen excerpts (16–32 measures) of increasing difficulty in five areas of percussion study: mallet, snare, timpani, auxiliary, drum set.

**SERVES:**
All percussion students.

1. **Establish a separate class for all percussionists.**
   Many directors have discovered the benefits of teaching percussion students independently of wind students. Directors are better able to focus on the unique challenges of percussion pedagogy while the percussionists can be featured in the percussion ensemble all year. Percussion students tend to be challenged and more on-task in percussion class than in a traditional band rehearsal. The most obvious concern with a percussion class is that the percussion section is not able to rehearse with the band regularly. Experience has shown that having a couple of sectionals on the band music during percussion class and having the percussion section rehearse two or three times with the band is sufficient to prepare for a concert. Though there is a great deal of challenging percussion writing in the modern wind repertoire, percussionists generally have easier part assignments than their wind counterparts. The benefits of the percussion class seem to greatly outweigh the inconveniences.

2. **Establish "Levels" for Mallet, Snare, Timpani, Auxiliary, and Drum Set.**
   Set an expectation of a balanced approach to all percussion instruments. Every percussion student studies all percussion instruments. Specialists are not allowed. (Our percussionists do not play the same instrument more than once with the band on the concert.) The percussion class curriculum is based on a series of sixteen excerpts or "levels" in five areas of percussion study: mallet, snare, timpani, auxiliary, and drum set. The levels can be 16 to 32 measures long and should increase in difficulty. Levels may be obtained from existing sources, such as *Audition Etudes*, by Garwood Whaley, or *Balanced Percussion Education*, by David Fullmer and Kevin Meyer. Or, they may be composed to match the skill levels of your students.

3. **Set aside a day or two every five weeks for levels testing.**
Each member of the percussion class is expected to "pass off" two levels every five weeks—once at mid-term and again at the end of the term. The students can choose which levels to prepare, as long as they meet the following two criteria:

   * The levels must be passed off in sequential order (no skipping around).
   * The students cannot get more than two levels ahead in any one category.

These simple criteria ensure each student's balanced approach to percussion study. Students must earn an A (performance-ready) or B (a few minor problems) in order for the level to be passed off. Students earning a C or lower must redo the level at the next testing session. The levels grade average counts for one third of the final grade. (Performance attendance and practice are the other two thirds.) It is not uncommon for some students to pass off more than the required two. While the order and speed students learn the levels will be different, each one is progressing in all five areas of percussion.

4. **Record test results on the percussion ranking sheet.**
List each student and the last level passed off in each of the five areas. This helps students plan for the next testing session and helps the teacher ensure that the two criteria mentioned in step 3 have been met by each student. Give each student one point for every level successfully passed off. Students are then ranked based on the points earned. Point ties are broken by the following:

   * number of levels passed off
   * average grade of levels passed off
   * previous ranking

With these tie-breakers, the entire percussion class can be ranked. The rankings have several purposes. Students ranked 1–8 comprise the percussion section for the top band and orchestra. Students ranked 9–14 comprise the percussion section for the second band. This has eliminated time-consuming auditions and made the selection of these sections completely objective. It has also eliminated the feeling of entitlement commonly found in some upper classmen. The rankings are also used when distributing parts for percussion ensembles. The number-one ranked player gets first choice, number two gets second choice, etc. Remember, the rankings can change every five weeks. It is important for the director to teach the purposes of the rankings and create an atmosphere where the students are mutually supportive in their study.

5. **Enjoying the benefits of a well-balanced percussion class curriculum.**
Our percussionists begin class together everyday with a warm-up (alternate mallets and stick and pad) and sight-reading. The remaining class time is used depending on the needs of the day. The director may choose to rehearse the concert band percussion section, teach those who have not passed off the first drum set level, have the section leader rehearse the marching band battery while the director rehearses the front line section, or rehearse one of the concert percussion ensembles for an upcoming festival. The options are as numerous and varied as the performance requirements of an active music department. Many of these choices would not include the entire class at one time. Herein lies one of the greatest benefits of the levels curriculum: even if a project does not involve every member of the class, every member of the class has something to work on. This recipe is easily adaptable to fit the needs of any school. *Bon appetit!* �➤

# Commissioning a New Work of Music

*David R. Gillingham*

Commissioning a new work of music is a project that many music directors are reluctant to pursue, because they do not know where to begin. Following a step-by-step process will render a quintessential experience for all parties involved.

**INGREDIENTS:**
Funds for the project, to cover the commissioning fee, residency costs, and any other miscellaneous costs associated with the project. Supportive parents, community, and administration.

**SERVES:**
All music students, the director(s), parents, administrators, and the community.

### STEP 1. Choose the composer.
When choosing a composer, the *sponsor* (person or persons commissioning the composer) should be familiar with that composer's music. Don't choose a composer on the suggestion of another music director or musician or because the composer is a "big name" and it seems "fashionable" to choose this particular composer at this particular time. Choose the composer for the sole reason that his/her music speaks to you in a special way. If the sponsor plans on doing a consortium commission, the primary sponsor will have to discuss possible choices with the members of the consortium and come to unanimous agreement on the choice of a composer.

### STEP 2. Set the budget.
The budget for a commission should cover the commissioning fee, copying costs (if applicable), residency fees (travel, lodging, food, and per diem charges), and any other miscellaneous expenses related to the project. The sponsor can "guesstimate" the cost of the commission by the following dollar amounts, which are per *minute* of music. This will vary from composer to composer.

|  |  |
|---|---|
| $1000 | Large ensemble work: orchestra, band, wind ensemble, chamber orchestra, orchestra/band with soloist |
| $500 | Choir with accompaniment or a cappella |
| $250 | Solo works |

If the sponsor is involved in a consortium, then the total amount is divided equally among the membership.

### STEP 3. Contact the composer.

The sponsor can contact the composer in person or by phone, letter, or e-mail. Do this *well in advance* of the projected premiere of the proposed new work, with the minimum being one year. Most established composers are booked several years ahead and the sponsor may need to be flexible about the premiere date. Ask the composer about availability, willingness, financial details, the type of work, instrumentation, and the timetable for residencies and completion. It should be noted that most composers require half or at least a portion of the commissioning fee down, as soon as there is an agreement in writing.

### STEP 4. Put it in writing.

Put the details of the commission agreement in writing, with all parties signing and retaining copies. Some composers have their own standard contract that spells out every conceivable detail. Other details to consider might be the ownership of the piece and rights to performances for a certain time period (usually a year) before the publication of the piece. Also, the publisher of the work might want rights to recordings to be used for promotional purposes. The contract should also include commissioning information that will be placed on the title page of the score. Some sponsors like to have this information included on individual parts, as well.

### STEP 5. Arrange for a pre-composition mini-residency.

Since the work will be specifically tailored for the students and the director, it makes perfect sense for the sponsor and the composer to get to know one another. During this time, the composer can familiarize the students and the director with more of his or her music and talk about his or her philosophy of music. It will also enable the sponsors to ask questions and offer suggestions for the type of piece they have in mind.

### STEP 6. The creative period.

The work is now upon the shoulders of the composer in the ensuing months to complete the composition. It will be assumed that the composer and sponsor(s) will remain in close contact in case any questions arise.

### STEP 7. Completion.

Score and parts are delivered to the sponsor. The sponsor pays the remaining commissioning fee to the composer. The time frame for paying the composer should be specified in the contract.

### Step 8. Rehearsals and mini-residency.

During the final rehearsals, or perhaps before, the composer should be invited for a mini-residency. The composer's input during these rehearsals is extremely vital.

### STEP 9. The premiere.

Make certain that the composer is present for the premiere. In some cases, the composer may wish to conduct the premiere performance. (All the more reason for the mini-residency.) It is also helpful if the composer talk briefly about the work before the performance. This is a big event! Savor each moment for what it is worth. ➥

# Program Planning

*Steven Grimo*

Selecting your program order is a creative process that will enhance your ensemble presentation. When the right order of compositions is presented, your performance will be most enjoyable to your audience. Creative thought concerning what the audience hears, sees, and experiences, from an emotional standpoint, is a recipe for a successful culinary delight.

**INGREDIENTS:**
Well-thought-out program options—using your program database with your favorite selections. You can mix and match various styles and music categories, which will enhance your total presentation.

**SERVES:**
Will serve all audience and ensemble members with musical satisfaction and enjoyment.

### From Cutting Board to Serving Dish—Repertoire to Selection
As you prepare this fine meal, programming must whet the listening appetite of the audience. A well-balanced program will enhance all emotional and creative senses in the same way that a world-renowned chef prepares his table with exotic delights. Create a database with all your favorite selections. Include categories such as overtures, marches, suites, symphonies, show medleys, contemporary works, and encores—and be sure to include the time and style of each selection. You will then be able to sort and select from a variety of options by setting up your own recipe box.

### From Market to Home—Rehearsal to Stage
Of course, each meal must be accompanied by wines that complement and desserts that tantalize. The total effect will be you as the connoisseur—the metamorphosis of a conductor as transformed from master chef to composer. Yes, with you as the composer of this program, you will present your ensemble as a fine menu of musical expression. The personality, heart, and soul of everyone performing should speak through your musical selections. Every part of your musical event is a performance, from the first person who enters the stage to the final performers who exit.

### From Kitchen to Table—Performer to Audience
A program formula can have many different facets: with intermission or without, an opening welcome with narrated program notes or simply printed notes for the audience to think and

reflect upon. Your intermission can be the division between challenging and easy listening. Your entire program can be enhanced with marches and lighter selections. The length of a program can be anywhere from 45 minutes on each side to a 50-minute first half and 35-minute second half, which works well from a listening standpoint. Your planning should also include talking and program notes relative to music performance.

### Ingredients and Program Planning

**First consideration.** Open your performance with a selection that brings attention and that is exciting and brilliant. It does not have to be loud and technical, but should show command of performance and confidence. It should project a sense of "welcome to our performance!" Overtures, dance movements, and marches work well as opening selections. Remember that the audience has not quite settled down to think of what is on the menu yet . . . they will also be making judgments on what is being served and what may be in store for them throughout the program. Allow them to relax and settle in.

**Second consideration.** Your most reflective work on the program can be presented at this point. Your audience can now digest and enjoy a fine soloist and thought-provoking work. This will be challenging for the performers and audience alike. Brilliant featured soloists, tone poems, folk song settings, or symphonic suites are now ready for presentation.

**Third and final consideration.** This will be the most ambitious selection on the program. This is the time for your major symphonic work, newly commissioned project to be premiered, or guest composer/conductor presenting their composition—something to which your ensemble has dedicated their hearts and souls. Then, begin the gradual relaxation from challenging to easy listening selections, which will appeal to your audience and allow them to enjoy and reflect what they have just experienced. *Relax and prepare for dessert*: several selections that will be totally for the audience's pleasure alone.

### Cooking with Balance and Moderation

The repertoire chosen must be challenging and not discouraging. Include a variety of light and heavy selections, old and new, fast and slow, loud and soft, reflective and dramatic. Keep your thought process simple. Allow emotions to be part of your presentation, and perform with excitement and conviction.

Your careful consideration of how tempo, key relationships, and reflective moods are presented to the audience will enhance your overall musical presentation. Prepare your audience for an emotional and reflective response. It may range from serious reflection to exuberant and enjoyable laughter.

### Setting the Table and Communication

A less formal atmosphere can be best for many performances. The use of an announcer keeps the audience engaged and attentive. This also gives the performers a rest between selections to mentally get ready for the next piece. There is a need for time between pieces, and we tend to move on to the next selection without adequate time to prepare and reflect on the next mood or expression to be presented, both from a performer's and audience's standpoint. If you choose not to have program notes presented by an announcer, do consider leaving the stage between compositions and allow for applause and time for the performers to prepare for the next selection.

Programming need not be difficult. If you prepare and plan, your menu will always be exciting and enjoyable. Develop a program format that works for your ensemble. Here is a sample program menu:

## OVERTURE

An aperitif to tantalize and challenge the appetite.

## MARCH

Hors d'oeuvres to stimulate and relax the soul.

## A BRILLIANT SOLOIST

A salad course with a rare-tasting dressing that will enhance curiosity and taste.

## SYMPHONY, CONTEMPORARY WORK, BALLET SUITE

A solid main course of whatever suits our creativity for the day.

*Intermission*

## FRESH SUGGESTION: BE DARING

A vegetable that we don't really like but know is good for us.

## LIGHT AND RELAXING WORK, EASY TO DIGEST

A fruit or cheese course to cleanse and clear the palate.

## A SELECTION THAT BRINGS PLEASURE

A sweet and delectable dessert, or festive flambeau. ➤●

# Well-Rounded Teaching and Balanced Learning Outcomes

*Alan Gumm*

Contrary to the notion that there is one single effective way to teach music, there are instead various ways to effectively accomplish learning outcomes. The outcomes intended by the conductor before the rehearsal guide every action in the rehearsal. This poem is offered to help in making purposeful choices for the types of outcomes that fit your personal music teaching style and the types of approaches that match the desired outcome.

**INGREDIENTS:**
Three components in the teaching/learning process: (a.) a teacher, (b.) students of all types and characteristics, (c.) an organized set of music content and outcomes.

**SERVES:**
All instrumental and voice students.

The skills of teaching are many; be conscious of choices you make.
To teach **narrowly** or **well rounded**, you must know the options at stake.

For students to **follow directions** you give, state your aim as a doable task.
Turn your eyes, ears, and mind to check each one's success, and point out when they do what you ask.

Further yet is to **hold their attention at length**, which takes an intense visual stance.
Express with your face, move about, shift the pace, and keep them alert with a glance.

A quick use of time and multiple tasks will **cover more ground** in the day.
Have students stay actively occupied, and be brief in all that you say.

Most important of all is to **make learning fun**, not for laughs, but to show your concern.
Show praise and approval at signs of success, and let patience prevail as they learn.

There is more to this learning than following your lead—work in groups to let go of strict rule.
Build **leadership, teamwork, and self-governance**, which are skills that they'll need beyond school.

Teaching **depth of knowledge** turns "teaching" around to ask students to think on their own.
The more they compare and choose for themselves, the deeper you know they have grown.

The **experience and senses** of sight, feel, and sound that only skilled experts can yield
are described, modeled, imaged, and allegorized until students, too, master the field.

**Innovation and personal insight**—beyond viewpoints that others possessed—
are brought out through dialogue, not lecture, and nurtured through acceptance, not tests.

You see, teaching depends on the outcome you want, so choose wisely your aim and intent:
to conform to your thoughts, find out for themselves, recall, analyze, or invent. ➟●

# The Great Musical Adventure: Commissioning Music for School Ensembles

*Frederick Harris, Jr.*

"If we are to leave any musical legacy for the future, it will be because we give more of our efforts and time to music of our own age." — Don Moses

Engaging students in the process of bringing a piece of music to life that has been composed especially for them is among the most powerful educational experiences. The opportunity to interact with a composer not only heightens their appreciation for composition, but also inspires them to explore their own creativity. To "commission" a composer means to pay the composer for creating a piece of music. But funding should not deter you from exploring the development of your own commissioning project. There are many avenues to use in approaching this enriching idea.

**INGREDIENTS:**
**Dream.** Your imagination is the driving force behind the project.

**Composer exploration.** The musical and personal integrity of the composer is key.

**Budget development.** Identify and explore all possible resources.

**Project development.** Establish an educational philosophy behind the project.

**Project implementation.** Prepare your students for the experience, the piece, and the composer.

**Evaluation and continuation.** Nurture a creative culture.

**SERVES:**
All music education students and their teachers at every level.

**The Six Steps**
  **1.  Dream.** Your imagination is the driving force behind the project.
Allow yourself to become excited at the prospect of a composer writing a work for your students: the sense of adventure, the challenges, the composer interacting with you and your students, and the feeling at the concert when you present the first performance. Consider the strengths and weaknesses of your ensemble. Are there sections or soloists that may be featured? Are there particular musical aspects to which you would like to expose students, such as improvisation or free rhythm? Is there a collaborative opportunity to explore, such

as a work for elementary chorus and high school percussion ensemble? You don't want to restrict a composer, but he or she may be interested in your ideas and may help tailor the piece to your specific ensemble.

2. **Composer exploration.** The musical and personal integrity of the composer is *key*. It's essential that you spend quality time choosing a composer. Be certain to listen to the composer's music of all genres, not just the one you want him to write for. (Chamber music is often the most telling.) Consider composers who may not have composed for the genre you want. It may be more interesting than commissioning someone who has already written one hundred compositions for your chosen genre. Ask yourself the following: Does the composer have a record of quality compositions? Would the composer interact well with my students? Don't be afraid to explore collegiate student composers. Also, contact composers at least one or two years before you want the piece. The more experienced the composer, the further ahead you should contact them—as much as four to five years, in some cases.

3. **Budget development.** Identify and explore all possible resources.
Consider all the internal resources available, such as school funds, PTA, parent groups, parents associated with businesses, etc., as well as external resources such as local and state arts grants. It's important to always align requests for funding with the educational mission of the project. Also, consider collaborating with other schools in a consortium. You can split the cost of the project, and the composer gets multiple performances of the piece. Everybody wins!

4. **Project development.** Establish an educational philosophy behind the project.
The possibilities for the creative engagement of the students beyond rehearsing and performing the piece are vast. Consider the curricula implications inherent in such a project, such as units on compositional techniques, composer biographies, and related interdisciplinary areas such as visual art. Any way that you can involve members of the faculty and community will help to create contagious excitement for the project. Have your goals and an outline of the project in writing and use it to educate parents, students, and community about what you are doing.

5. **Project implementation.** Prepare your students for the experience, the piece, and the composer.
As soon as you have a verbal agreement with the composer over the length of the piece and its due date, you must have a written contract that outlines all aspects of the commission, including composer visitations, attendance at the premiere, the cost of copying parts, and when and how he or she will be paid. The extent to which you prepare your students for this project will largely determine its success. Do they have an awareness of the process of composition? Have they learned about the composer? Have you engaged members of the school and outside community in some facet of the project? Have you considered all the details for the presentation of the piece on the concert, i.e., should the composer speak? Do the local and statewide media know about the project?

6. **Evaluation and continuation.** Nurture a creative culture.
It is important to evaluate the project once it's completed. Consider having students maintain journals with their observations of the entire process. Seek input about the project from the composer as well as from your colleagues. While it may not be possible to make commissioning an annual endeavor, consider doing it every few years so that students will have the experience at least once while attending your school. The enlightenment of students, parents, and community members of the value of this kind of educational experience will create the foundation for its continuation into the future. ➺

# Ensuring Success When Matching Beginners with Instruments

*Samuel R. Hazo*

Assigning beginning students to the proper instruments can be the guarantee of a quality band program through twelfth grade. Unfortunately, the reciprocal is also true. Poor instrument assigning with beginners is such a serious issue that the program might not recover from mistakes made in the early years. Therefore, here are some helpful hints to make sure that your first attempts set the program in the right direction.

**INGREDIENTS:**
Woodwind instruments, brass instruments, percussion instruments, young students, and a band director.

**SERVES:**
Band students and teachers.

**Rule No. 1.** The teacher decides which instrument is the perfect match for the student—not the student and not the parent. Just because the family has an old trumpet in the house doesn't give that child the license to play it. Also, you will have children approach you and say, "I want to play the trumpet and nothing else." To which your response must be:

> Well, if you pass the trumpet examination, great! If not, we'll try some other instruments until we find the right match. I would not like you to become frustrated playing an instrument that is difficult for you because of something you can't help, like maybe the shapes we have to make with our mouths will be uncomfortable for you. We all want music to be fun and rewarding. So, we're not going to assign you an instrument that will be frustrating, even if it is the one that is your first choice.

Do not give in, or you will regret it from the very first lesson!

**Rule No. 2.** The proper sound on each instrument must be modeled for the beginning auditioners by you, another teacher, or a proficient older student, before students attempt it themselves. No amount of verbal instruction can take the place of that beginning child initially hearing the instrument's proper sound.

**Rule No. 3.** If the child does not get the proper sound within the first thirty seconds, having had quality instruction in the try-out from you and the proper auditory modeling, odds are that he or she might not ever do it. Time to move on to the next instrument.

Here are some accompanying qualifications for each instrument that will help.

## WOODWINDS

### Flute

- The student must make the proper sound on the head joint (around an A natural), with one hand covering the open end. If the sound is "airy" for any other reason than their embouchure not being centered with the hole, the flute might not be the right match.
- The student can not have a "teardrop" upper lip—otherwise known as a "widow's peak." The air will divide around the airhole, and it will sound like a Coke bottle forever.
- Have each student repeat several fine motor exercises that you make up and model first. Going from an open hand to the "Live long and prosper" sign from Star Trek is a good one. If a simple fine motor exercise seems to be too challenging, learning the flute could be very frustrating in terms of fine motor skill demands.

### Oboe and Bassoon

- I hate to say it this way, but intelligence and desire play big parts with these two instruments. Have you ever met a good double-reed player who is lacks intellegence? Told you so.
- Of great importance with the oboe and bassoon is the student's hand size (reach), dexterity, and finger strength.
- Insist that oboe and bassoon students take additional private lessons outside of school because these are such complex instruments.
- Hand-made reeds should be the priority choice if there is a private teacher available in the area who can make them. Because these reeds are so expensive, take great concern in choosing students whose families will not be burdened by this expense if the school district doesn't cover the cost. Tell parents about the reed costs up front.
- These are great transfer instruments for strong clarinet and saxophone players who can produce a good double-reed sound.

### Clarinet

- This is the single-reed instrument on which most students should begin, even those interested in the saxophone. Clarinet provides the greatest basis from which students can switch to another reed instrument.
- Make sure students can flatten their chin, blow hot air, and play down to a thumb and six-fingered G. Turn the neck and mouthpiece around so that the child can blow into the instrument, and you, the teacher, can face the student and finger the notes. Have the student hold the neck so the instrument doesn't jam into his or her mouth.
- Students whose sound gets thicker and louder as they play down to a low G would transfer easily to the bass clarinet after a few months.
- Overbites and especially under bites can cause difficulty in some cases, so keep an eye on their mouth structure.

### Saxophone (Alto for Beginners)

* So many students can get a sound out of a saxophone that only the students who get the perfect dark tone from the beginning should be placed on this instrument.
* Make sure students can duplicate simple fine motor exercises that you create and model for them. They must feel comfortable with their dexterity because, unlike clarinet players, saxophone students cannot peripherally see their fingers.
* Pronounced overbites and underbites can cause great difficulty with the saxophone, because proper mouthpiece position is just about perpendicular to the chin, and the upper and lower teeth should align.

## Brass

We must make our brass players sing! Start when they're young, when they'll do it without hesitation.

### Trumpet

* Look at the teeth. Preferably, there should be a high point somewhere in front, on which you can place the mouthpiece. A slight gap between the teeth or angled bottom edges can be of additional help. Students with flat, straight teeth probably will have difficulty attaining and then maintaining the upper register for extended periods of time.
* There is a myth that students with full lips cannot play the trumpet or French horn. This is not true. Everything depends on how thin the embouchure portion of the lips can get while in the playing position.
* The student must be able play an open G with very little effort. From there, students should be able to blow faster and slower air to produce the open Cs above and below the middle G. (You must model all three pitches first.)
* Students who can match pitch and sing simple solfège passages back to you have an easier time finding the proper lip positions (Do-Re-Mi-Re-Do, Do-Mi-Sol-Mi-Do, Sol-Do-Sol).

### French Horn

* Follow the same points as with trumpet. However, this is more difficult on French horn, so if a student gets the proper horn sound and can still hit the low, middle, and high open notes (C-G-C), you have a real find.
* French horn students must be able to sing these simple solfège passages back to you, on pitch: Do-Re-Mi-Re-Do, Do-Mi-Sol-Mi-Do, Sol- Do-Sol. Their ability to sing pitches translates into how well they will find their lip positions.
* Like the oboe and bassoon, an additional weekly private lesson outside of school is imperative.

### Trombone/Baritone

* Students must be able play a middle F with very little effort. From there, students must be able to blow faster and slower air to produce the B-flats above and below the middle F. (You must model all three pitches first.)
* Trombone players must be able to sing back pitches: Do-Re-Mi-Re-Do, Do-Mi-Sol-Mi-Do, Sol-Do-Sol. Their musical ear should be instinctive in order to control the infinite variables of the slide.
* Students who produce results on this size mouthpiece, but who are more comfortable with fine motor movement or who have less arm length than needed for the trombone, will fare well on the baritone/euphonium. The baritone is also a great

transfer from the trumpet for students whose low trumpet register surpasses their upper register.

## Tuba

Follow the same points as trombone and baritone, as well as those below.

- Generally, this is a great transfer instrument for students who started on baritone and trombone. But don't rule out clarinet, sax, and trumpet players whose facial growth patterns lend themselves to the size of a tuba mouthpiece.
- If your school system starts band students in fourth grade, you will have fewer students who can produce the Do-Sol-Do (B-flat-F-B-flat) pattern on the tuba than in schools that start band in sixth grade. It is an instrument that lends itself to larger lungs and mouth structure.
- Do your best to own a smaller sized tuba—termed "three-quarter sized"—for the young child. This helps greatly in dealing with the cumbersome qualities of the instrument.

## Percussion

- The percussion students should be the most innately musical students you can find. Band teachers who put the weakest students on percussion are the same ones who complain that the percussion method book is too hard. (Hint: It's not the method book!)
- Students must be able to clap three patterns back to you with absolute precision. Start with one of medium difficulty. Include a half note to measure their internal tempo. Then, try a hard one, then a really hard one with syncopation. Accept only those students who repeat all three patterns note for note and at the same tempo as you modeled.
- It is imperative that we start students on melodic as well as non-melodic percussion. (Piano players adapt incredibly well.) As they grow with the program, the percussion repertoire demands will increase faster than those of other instruments. Grade 2 percussion pieces are still mainly for snare drum, bass drum, cymbals, and glockenspiel. At grade 3, this jumps to every instrument you can own with intricate playing responsibilities. You will need to have true musicians who can handle these challenges. ➤●

# Teaching Principles of Melodic Interpretation

*Leslie W. Hicken*

Melody is one of the primary elements found in music from all historical periods. Interpreting a musical phrase is the first step in cultivating individual artistic expression. However, many fundamentals of melodic interpretation are addressed using a less than systematic approach. Often, students will not interpret melody unless prompted by specific instructions from the composer or their music director. If we can teach our students to interpret melody beyond the symbols that are utilized on the page, true artistry and creativity can be fostered. This approach takes principles learned from the private studio experience and applies them to the large ensemble environment.

**INGREDIENTS:**
Various digital scale patterns. Chorales and unison melodies. Sequential application of the following principles to the literature studied.

**SERVES:**
All instrumental and voice students.

When reading a score or performing an ensemble piece, chamber music, or solo composition, the interpretation principles that I learned as a young clarinetist quickly fall into place. It is as if I am hearing the music through the musical point of view of my clarinet teacher. Stanley Hasty taught me to interpret the music beyond what was notated on the page through various principles that can be applied to any melodic passage. I have tried to teach these principles to my students in my role as a large ensemble director. If we can train our students to interpret music the way we do, we can create a synergistic musical environment in which everyone is contributing to the music making process.

The first principle is very basic. In a melodic passage, you crescendo when notes ascend and decrescendo when the pitches descend. We call this "shaping the phrase." Many times composers expect this to happen naturally, even though they do not specifically notate this in their music. Great musicians do this intuitively. We can train our students to do this through simple digital scale patterns (e.g., 1-2-3-4-5-4-3-2-1) played legato during our warm-up sequences.

The second principle is that melodic sustained tones or repeated notes must not remain static; they either crescendo or decrescendo. The decision as to which would be accomplished will be made within the context of the musical phrase. You can have your ensemble alternate repeated eighth notes and whole notes on various scale degrees. Each repetition can apply either a crescendo or decrescendo to the sustained or repeated note.

The third principle deals with *expressive upward intervals*. It is helpful to imagine a great violinist making a melodic leap of an octave in an expressive passage. The technique that they use to connect the notes of the interval is called *portamento*. As wind players, we cannot slide into these upward pitches; glissando is not the desired effect here. However, we can connect these notes by increasing the air pressure on the bottom note and allowing the upper note to appear at the top of the interval. A good way to train this is to play diatonic intervals up from tonic. What you are listening for is a strong lower note that leads to the upper pitch of the interval accomplished with no break in the sound. Additionally, you do not allow the upper note to crescendo out of context relative to timbre or dynamic. This is a powerful principle to enhance expressive melodic interpretation.

The fourth principle deals with the concept of ebb and flow in the music, which we call *tension and release*. Using chorales, you can illustrate this principle by isolating dominant seventh chord to tonic cadences. The idea is to crescendo through the dominant seventh chord in the phrase and then release tension on the cadence to tonic with a decrescendo. This gives the musical phrase momentum and a sense of direction. Even using unison scales, you can point out how the seventh scale degree resolving to the eighth degree adds this sense of tension to the musical line. The same can be felt when the fourth scale degree resolves down to the third.

Although there are other concepts that can be applied to musical interpretation (for instance, note lengths and tapering of phrases), these first four principles can open up a whole new world of expression and musicality. If students actively respond to the music that they study using this recipe, the rehearsal can become an environment in which each performer explores personal musical imagination and creativity. ➤●

# Why Did We Play That? Selecting Music and Methodology to Meet a Wide Variety of Needs

*Roy C. Holder*

As we decide what our students will rehearse each day, it is necessary to first decide exactly what it is we are interested in teaching. Simply programming "quality literature" will not in and of itself ensure that we are meeting the needs of everyone involved. Our choice of materials becomes not only our curriculum, but also our means of communicating with the world outside our rehearsal room.

**INGREDIENTS:**
Scale sheets, rhythm reading exercises, method books, music for sight-reading, performance literature, and recordings.

**SERVES:**
All music students.

In the early stages of learning to perform music, we often rely heavily on one or more of the published method book series as the guide to what will happen in class each day. Though no single source can meet all the needs of every individual student, this approach has the advantage of exposing every student to a matching set of knowledge and skills. A tuba player, a trombone player, or a percussionist playing mallets can learn to read eighth note passages at the same time as a flute or violin player. Even in the early stages, however, simply working through the book will not guarantee that the clarinets learned the proper chromatic fingerings or that the flutes learned to play in the top octave. Developing the wide variety of specialized skills necessary for success on every instrument requires careful planning from the very beginning.

Continuing this development as students progress becomes even more tedious. The use of rhythm and method books can help students develop certain skills, but without quality literature to perform, this soon becomes pointless. As we progress to more literature and less methodology, skill development becomes more difficult. Marches, for example, are an important part of our heritage, and should be programmed regularly. Very few of these, however, are great for developing technique in the French horn section. There are many wonderful compositions that challenge the treble instruments while completely ignoring the low voices and percussionists. There are even many fine works that help us teach advanced musicianship skills but do not inspire many of the ensemble members to run home and practice, because personal practice of the notes is not really the issue.

It quickly becomes obvious that no single composition is necessarily going to meet all the developmental needs of every performer. Selecting a variety of material designed to meet predetermined needs becomes imperative. If we want tuba and trombone players with technical skills, it is necessary to give them something challenging that they will enjoy playing—such as a march with a great break strain or even one of the great circus marches. If we expect the horns to develop range and technique, they need to have a part that challenges them technically. In fact, if we do not provide each student material that they must work to accomplish, we should not be too surprised when they do not practice. By the same logic, if a student never plays a composition that requires them to stretch their phrasing and musicality skills, they will probably not become very proficient in these areas.

If we expect our students to develop the wide range of skills necessary to fine performance, it is necessary for us to first decide exactly what these skills are, evaluate our current musicians for strengths and weaknesses, and then set about the task of selecting a wide variety of materials designed to help each individual and section acquire and improve the selected skills. Only by knowing in advance what we want to accomplish and carefully selecting a variety of methods and literature to match can we hope to develop outstanding musicians. (Of course we can select a wonderfully planned curriculum and still not succeed if we do not carefully follow through with high expectations for every student, but that is an entirely different discussion.)

The great secondary benefit of selecting a highly varied set of music designed to meet the individual technical and musical needs of every musician, is that this variety also helps design programs that are interesting to the audience. By selecting material that offers technical challenges to the tubas, the percussionists, and all of the other sometimes forgotten individuals, we also provide the audience with a wide variety of instrumentations to keep them involved. By selecting material from several time periods in order to teach a variety of styles, we obviously provide the audience with a variety of styles. And by selecting material that also requires great melodic interpretation we provide moments of relaxation within the performance. If we can now manage to order these selections in a manner that provides a constant tension and release for both performers and audience, we just might intrigue our students, teach the desired musical skills, *and* win the hearts of our audience. ➤

# The Pitch Barometer — Measuring Intonation Skills

*Shelley Jagow*

Monitoring the pitch accuracy of players in a large ensemble is especially difficult when we are often limited in our rehearsal time. How then do we measure the pitch-matching skills of each and every player in our group? Does this sound like a formidable task? It doesn't have to be. Try this recipe to evaluate your student's intonation skills.

**INGREDIENTS:**
Ensure that instruments are properly warmed up before making this recipe. Players should be able to play a few basic scales and identify and perform various intervals in the scale key.

**SERVES:**
All instrumental and voice students.

It is impossible, and quite frankly a waste of time, to go around the room with a tuner to every player. Even if you had the time during a rehearsal to do this, you really have only assured yourself of one thing—you can be somewhat comfortable knowing that every player is at least close to sounding in tune on a unison concert B-flat, or whichever concert note you decide to tune. However, there is never any guarantee that the players will all sound this close to tune on any other note they play during rehearsal. We all understand that each brand/ make and type of wind instrument comes packaged with its own intonation tendencies. Just as no two snowflakes are ever identical, so too are no two saxophones or two horns, etc. ever truly identical in how they sound pitch.

Singing with your band and orchestra is an effective method to improving both tone quality and intonation. Young musicians invariably play with a better tone and sense of pitch immediately after singing a passage. Warm-up routines can be created to include singing as a regular activity. Singing intervals and scales develops an increased awareness of pitch and interval relationships. The best way to be able to play intervals in tune is to be able to sing intervals in tune. In addition, there are advantages to singing motifs and melodies in current repertoire that the ensemble is preparing. Singing also has merit for rehearsing rhythmic precision. The more practice we have at singing intervals, the better able we will be in the audition process before actually sounding the note.

Students should first practice playing unisons in tune, followed by open octave intervals, then perfect fifths, major thirds, and minor thirds. The concept of balance comes into play when recognizing and tuning intervals. In other words, students must remember to fit the higher sounding notes into the lower sounding notes. Once the correct balance is achieved, it is much easier to recognize the interval and make appropriate adjustments.

Now it is time to use your Pitch Barometer. Here is how it works. Periodically monitor pitches of individual players by instructing the entire ensemble to sustain a unison pitch and then point to one player to continue sustaining the pitch while the other players release their sound. (Strive to create a friendly learning atmosphere while using the Pitch Barometer, because it does place less confident players on the spot.) The lone sounding pitch will immediately sound sharp, flat, or in tune with the released pitch.

You may be wondering how this is so when surely the entire section was not accurately matching accurate pitch. The reason this pitch barometer technique works so well is because the sum of the parts equals the whole. In other words, the whole sound moves to the closet in-tune pitch. Allow the players to determine the relation of their pitch to the whole, while encouraging them to follow their first instinct. If we think too long on the direction of our pitch, then our ears can be easily confused and not know which direction to move at all. The goal is for a student to independently and instantly identify pitch relations and make immediate adjustments. Using the Pitch Barometer a few seconds at every rehearsal will certainly involve students more actively with their ears! ➞●

# Preserving Your Musicians

*William Jastrow*

From beginning grades through high school graduation and on into college, music educators face the difficult and frustrating challenge of recruiting and retaining students for elective music performance classes. At the same time, students, parents, and school officials face an ever-increasing smorgasbord of alternative activities and "educational" obstacles to participation in music. All too frequently, as a result of the misconception that music is a before-, after-, or lunch-time school activity on par with Little League or chess club, students drop band, orchestra, or choir, including students displaying strong interest and exceptional skills in music. Through a steady diet of information, this recipe nourishes students, parents, and administrators with the long-term creative, academic, and social benefits that cultural education through the study of music in an instrumental or vocal ensemble can provide.

**INGREDIENTS:**
Sample student schedules including GPAs, AP/ACT/SAT, college admission, and corporate statistics, quotes from alumni, parents, college admission officers, and corporate leaders, a list of state and national fine arts standards, a music education philosophy statement and an outline of goals and objectives, answers to frequently asked questions, examples of college music opportunities for non-majors, and a healthy spoonful of personal anecdotes. Most importantly, you must have an inspiring cookbook: *Strong Arts, Strong Schools*, by Charles Fowler (Oxford University Press).

This recipe, which requires multiple and diverse ingredients drawn from numerous resources, can be served in varying formats, such as personal letters, handouts, Power Point presentations, concert programs, and Web sites. It should be consumed with frequent regularity. Although designed for mass consumption, to be a "culinary" success, the final product must contain that "home baked for someone special" flavor.

**SERVES:**
Instrumental and vocal music students, parents, administrators, and school board and community members.

The first course should be served on Beginning Band and Orchestra Night. This evening should not focus on the selection of an instrument and a three-month rental contract, but rather on the exciting prospect of enrolling in a sequential, college preparatory music education program that strives to enrich cultural understanding, enhance creativity, and prepare students for various vocational or avocational experiences with the arts in the adult world. Ideally, this first course is catered by a team of elementary, middle, and high school music faculty. A Power Point presentation showing local students in high school or college ensembles combined with statistics on secondary music student test scores and quotes from college admissions officers and corporate executives can have a powerful impact on parents. Quarterly newsletters on the value of the arts, as well as involvement by area middle school, high school, or adult musicians in "Our First Concert" can reinforce the groundwork laid the first night and strengthen connections between the elementary music program and middle school music classes.

A difficult time for many music students and parents comes midway through eighth grade, with registration and enrollment for high school. Families are generally overwhelmed with information about graduation requirements, homework, class rank, college test preps, and AP credits, to say nothing of the myriad of school teams and activities. Although many students begin high school math or foreign language sequences while in seventh and eighth grade with the assumption that course work will continue in ninth grade, in the flood of high school information, students and parents frequently lose sight of music education as a parallel type of program.

Consequently, an abundant assortment of "Music Education Preserves" needs to reach both the parents and the student prior to the deluge from the guidance office. A mailing or e-mail during winter break, containing a personal invitation letter to enroll in the high school instrumental music education program and accompanied by a variety of support materials will all but guarantee that music reaches the dinner table first. Support materials can include the following documents:

- "Answers to Common Questions." Does a student need to continue instruction in music during high school if he or she does not plan to pursue that field professionally? How does participation in a high school music ensemble benefit a student when applying for college?
- Sample schedules of honor roll graduates that maintained a music elective throughout high school.
- "Who Will Be the Next Conductor of the Chicago Symphony?"—a compilation of stories about former students and their experiences with music in high school.

A well-crafted "jar of preserves" can dramatically communicate why music should remain part of a student's high school education and successfully demonstrate how a freshman can build a schedule around music, rather than trying to squeeze it in.

At all levels, advocacy for music education needs to be viewed as a daily activity. At every opportunity, faculty members, administrators, school board members, and community leaders should be offered tidbits of information relating to music education. Whether it is including the national standards in concert programs, developing detailed curriculum handouts for Back-to-School night, scheduling open rehearsals for parents, initiating cross-curriculum conversations with colleagues, sharing research information with the school board, or conversations with community leaders after the Memorial Day parade, the topic of music in the community and music education in the schools should always be on the menu.

Similarly, student musicians at all levels need an occasional taste of the musical experiences that lay on the horizon. Special entrees—such as a combined beginner and middle school band on the spring concert, an eighth grade Pizza and Pep Band night for a high school basketball game, a shared concert between a school ensemble and a local community music group, a district fine arts festival, or a performance by a college band, orchestra, choir, or jazz group at your school—can leave a lasting impression on both a young music student and a parent. A rehearsal room display of college pennants representing alumni that have continued on to perform in college ensembles, a bulletin board of university ensemble photographs including recent graduates, and concert programs highlighting seniors and their prospective colleges are all very proactive reminders about the role that music can play in a comprehensive secondary education of any student.

Pressure on high school students is enormous, particularly students entering junior year. The misconception that every student must take every honors/AP course offered while participating in multiple sports and community service programs in order to have an "acceptable" transcript for college literally scares some upperclassmen out of music. Therefore, it is essential that music educators consistently teach the value of music and the arts in general within the context of human civilization. Students and parents must be able to relate school music programs to college opportunities, career possibilities, employment skills, and adult art experiences.

Finally, a tempting dessert must be offered to seniors in regards to the potential music opportunities that await them in college, regardless of their major field of study. A letter to each senior containing remembrances of college and adult music experiences, a little personal encouragement, and some general information on how to contact a university conductor can go a long way towards extending your student's music education and involvement in music making for years to come.

# First There Was Tone

*Barry E. Kopetz*

Perhaps no other area of ensemble performance has more bearing on all other areas than the production of superior tone quality! And yet, how many directors approach the issue of tone quality through a warm-up that includes only the B-flat major scale and a short chorale? There is a better way, and it is not limited to "one" way to warm up an ensemble.

**INGREDIENTS:**

A proper warm-up will overcome a multitude of problems that the ensemble will encounter in the course of rehearsal. While there are many ways to do an ensemble warm-up, (which is different than an individual warm-up!), certain traits seem to be uniform among excellent teachers. They include, but are not limited to the following:

> First, the ensemble needs to play with characteristic tone quality.
> Second, the ensemble should attack and release together.
> Third, dynamics should be performed at a moderate level.
> Fourth, a consistent style of articulation must be developed.
> Fifth, good intonation must be observed at all times.
> Sixth, the ensemble must learn to breathe together.
> Seventh, the ensemble must follow the conductor.
> Eighth, the ensemble must play musically and expressively.

**SERVES:**

All instrumental and voice students.

Dealing with pitch problems as well as tone quality issues can take an inordinate amount of time during rehearsal, even in the very best ensembles. Addressing these issues during the course of the warm-up is both an efficient use of time and prepares students for the task of rehearsing the literature with the proper frame of mind.

Here is a method that seems to work. Require diligent, daily work on the "Eight Essentials of Ensemble Warm-up" each and every rehearsal in order to develop the maturity of tone quality and ensemble precision that is desired. It is absolutely necessary to focus upon each area in order for long-term improvement to take place, and the teacher must decide which of the areas require attention on a daily basis. It is strongly recommended that the teacher tell the ensemble *what* is being addressed when each selected exercise is played. In short, the students must invest in the warm-up if maximum benefit is to occur.

Play through exercises slowly at first, focusing carefully on note accuracy. Every pitch should be played at precisely the same time by every member of the ensemble. In unison exercises, allow all players with weaker embouchures to take higher notes down an octave. Stop often on notes that require an adjustment in pitch, and inform students how to listen for discrepancies and how to achieve correct intonation. There are no shortcuts. *Good pitch is not an accident!*

Vary the warm-up routine daily. Use normal articulation one day (*tah* or *too*), and a legato articulation another (*dah* or *doo*). Vary the tempo as accuracy improves. The key is to not trick the ensemble, but to train them to follow the conductor and to play with consistency. Have students mark pitches in need of tuning with an arrow pointing up or down as a reminder that an adjustment is necessary.

Precise, rapid articulation is developed slowly and patiently. Take the time (in sectional works just fine) to be certain that the stroke of the tongue is accurate, and that the quality of the releases are as good as the start of each tone—an oft missed concept! Use unison melodies, encouraging expressive playing from all ensemble members, mallets included, insisting that everyone watch the conductor and listen to each other at all times. Sensitivity to the conductor is an important part of the warm-up, and unison playing (and singing) helps to solve numerous problems that will be encountered while rehearsing ensemble literature. ➤●

# Dealing with Intonation

*Kenneth Laudermilch*

Good intonation is every bit as important to an ensemble as good tone. The two, in fact, are inseparably linked. Think about it; you never find one without the other or the absence of one and quality in the other. And yet intonation is frequently overlooked, even avoided, in our ensembles.

**INGREDIENTS:**
Be prepared to spend a bit more time with tuning in your next rehearsal and be willing to spot-check and linger on the intonation issue during subsequent rehearsals until the concept is firmly planted in students' subconscious minds. Talk about its importance in the overall scheme of music making. If you are a director who for one reason or another tends to avoid the issue, be vulnerable, roll up your sleeves, jump in, and lead the way.

**SERVES:**
All musicians in large or small ensembles.

Time may not be money for band directors as time is for other professionals, but it certainly will compromise the excellence of our music making if we allow it to. A good place to refuse the intimidation of the time crunch to achieve excellence would be at the beginning of every rehearsal during the tuning process. No other element of preparation is so important to sound, *ensemble*, and expression as intonation. The fact that from time to time we all have bad-ear days should not keep us from keeping ourselves and our students active and accountable in this regard. It is better to risk the embarrassment of making the wrong intonation call every now and then than to regularly sidestep the matter.

Begin by teaching students as early as elementary school that flabby pitches are flat pitches and that edgy pitches are sharp. (I do believe William Revelli deserves credit for that terminology.) Give them room for error. Tuning may take a few minutes longer in waiting for student responses, but the end result, teaching students to discriminate for themselves, is well worth it. If you are a particularly nurturing teacher who loves to give away the answers in the interest of saving time, you will have to exercise a measure of self-discipline with this approach. Teach your charges to trust their first impressions, as they are generally most reliable. You will find that elementary children can achieve 95 percent accuracy within just a few rehearsals as they sharpen their listening skills.

A strobe tuner is best used sparingly. Place it only in the hands of the person who will sound the tuning pitch. Passing the tuner down the line may be expedient but not conducive to good ear training. We want to engage the ears in this discerning process, not the eyes. Reading the VU meter may cause the student to make the necessary adjustment at the moment, while disengaging the ears for the remainder of the rehearsal.

Earlier we mentioned the relationship of intonation to tone. As students tune one at a time, they must also think about the tone they are producing. A tuning pitch should be round and warm with a good attack and release, never just a mere rendering of the pitch without respect to quality or shape. By settling into each rehearsal with foundational matters of intonation and tone at the forefront of our minds, we will better negotiate the myriad of notes, rhythms, and articulations headed our way. ➤●

# Why We Seek Excellence in Every Aspect of Teaching?

*Tim Lautzenheiser*

In our quest for musical excellence, we often have to beware of the "it's good enough" attitude that can become a barrier between the musicians and the goal of artistic expression.

**INGREDIENTS:**
An open mind, a caring heart, a desire for quality, a global understanding, an exemplary work ethic, a desire for ongoing improvement, and a sense of the immeasurable potential of a master teacher.

**SERVES:**
Our students and all those who are part of our band world.

It is so easy to become complacent in our evolving educational journey, and the personal inquiry of, "It's just fine as it is; why should we push any further?" starts to dominate all aspects of rehearsal preparation and performance standards. As a result, the musical possibilities are never realized, not because of the technical inabilities (and potential) of the ensemble, but because of the atmosphere of mediocrity that slowly but surely begins to accept "less than the best."

What is the value of pushing oneself to go above and beyond? Why should we strive to continue this ongoing self-improvement journey? What's the pay-off? Is it really worth all the effort? Perhaps these questions are best answered in the following quote by René Daumal:

> You cannot stay on the summit forever; you have to come down again. So why bother to go there in the first place? Just this; what is above knows what is below, but what is below does not know what is above. One climbs, one sees, one descends. One sees no longer, but one has seen. There is a way of conducting oneself in the lower regions by the memory of what one saw higher up. When one can no longer see, one can at least still know. We live and love by what we have seen.

The profundity in Mr. Daumal's writing is a bold reminder to all of us. We know we cannot be in *top form* at all times, however by focusing on "the summit"—a peak level of personal investment—we upgrade every aspect of life habits, even when we have those teaching days that are less than our best, and we can use the experience to make the necessary course corrections for the future.

73

The truly gifted educators understand the implications of their influence. They realize; *quality teaching isn't something you do; it is something you **are***. It becomes the primary professional (and personal) filter for all decision-making: *what will lift us all to a higher level of understanding and appreciation?*

Listening to great music reminds us what is worthy. Observing extraordinary teachers in action influences our own classroom expectations. Working with outstanding mentors keeps us focused on the priceless value of our art form. There is a way of conducting oneself in the lower regions by the memory of what one saw higher up. And so it is, and so it always will be.

Settle for nothing less than excellence; you and your students deserve it. ➤

# Jumping the Hurdles of Notation in Pursuit of Musical Freedom

*Edward S. Lisk*

Young musicians very seldom, if at all, venture out to discover musical sounds other than what is written. Their world of music making has been immersed in musical notation, method books, solos, and band music, without ever lifting an eye off the page of music. The following recipe provides a gateway into discovering the art of musical expression without notation. I share the following quote by notable teacher Eloise Ristad. Her words elevate the importance of such a musical experience.

> I use improvisation for many reasons. It can spark rich ideas for composition, for it gives us a more intimate sense of raw materials of sound. It provides an astonishing physical and emotional release, and helps develop the kind of spontaneity that can transform the way we play Bach or Mozart or Bartok. It creates a more direct personal relationship with an instrument that can melt square-shouldered bravado into keen-eared listening.

**INGREDIENTS:**
The recipe calls for a small group of students (six to ten) supported by a creative, imaginative band director. Total silence as each student contributes their mixture of melodic sounds to the beautiful composition that is being created by the entire group.

**SERVES:**
All instrumental students, from elementary to college levels, and directors. The recipe provides a healthy diet of musical vitamins to experience the truth and beauty of musical expression.

The beginning experiences of a young musician are best described as being consumed with the signs and symbols of musical notation. From day one, their eyes are keenly focused upon that huge circle called a whole note, followed by the little black block indicating a rest. As they focus on each note, they dare not take their eyes off the page for fear of mistakes. "Wow, this is neat, I can read music!"

As years pass, the young musician continues to turn the pages of method books, experiencing the complexities of notation while expanding their performance vocabulary. Young musicians very seldom, if at all (only scales), venture out to discover musical sounds other than what is written. In my travels as a clinician, I often ask a student (or director) to play a simple, beautiful lullaby. The response is always the same; the student is shocked to think I would request someone to play a song without music. I'm certain many of you have experienced a similar situation.

With this recipe, I introduce a procedure to eliminate fears of playing music without notation. To eliminate fears (both student and teacher), I replace the word "improvisation" with "free-form expression." Free-form expression provides young musicians with opportunities to exercise their musical imagination and creativity without musical notation.

The students discover the beautiful world of musical expression that exists beyond the boundaries of notes and rhythm patterns—the same kind of boundaries set by painting pictures by the number rather than spilling the colors beyond the lines. The important point to remember when presenting free-form expression is that everything the student plays is *correct!* You will find students hesitate to take the risk as they have only been conditioned to respond to notation or teacher directions. They frequently react with "I can't do this without music." Their first attempt will usually start with a line of rapid notes, and the melody becomes *busy* due to their nervousness in search for correctness. This is a natural reaction. It is very important not to make any corrections, only encourage experimenting with a line of notes. This is *their* entrance into *their* musical world, with the opportunity to shape melodic lines relative to *their* musical and performance experience. Believe and support their natural musical intelligence.

By removing some of these natural barriers and inhibitions (along with those taught), the student is free to drift in any melodic direction with any duration of notes providing a gateway into discovering the art of musical expression. The fewer notes played, the more freedom they have to listen and become involved with the *feeling* of pitch and note direction. Encourage long, flowing melodies in comfortable playing ranges to develop melodic coherency. This will guide them into a meaningful melody and build confidence in their very own creation. You will find that the longer the student plays a free-form melodic line, beauty and interest of the line will become increasingly apparent. *Their natural musical intelligence comes to life with musically cohesive thought and expression.*

When introducing this approach, you should not place any emphasis on key, time signature, or rhythm demands, as is the case with some current approaches to improvisation. Within a short period of time, your students will naturally experience success when playing free-form melodies and find the need for scale knowledge to expand their expressive possibilities.

Listed are several reasons for including this process as an important part of instrumental study for your students.

1. Free form expression is an opportunity to discover one's natural musical intelligence.
2. It provides an opportunity to release an individual's imagination and creativity through the sound of his or her musical instrument.
3. It allows students to become sensitive to the feeling of resolution—moving a pitch or a series of notes within a phrase from tension to resolution or point of repose, and feeling the direction of their artistic decision.
4. It provides a mind/body connection with the "soul" of the individual through the sound of an instrument (thinking and decision making). A departure from "contrived" musical expression or meaningless notes.
5. It provides opportunities to develop and exercise interpretation and stylistic performance. It is an opportunity to go beyond the written symbols of musical notation to faithfully experience the composer's musical intentions.

6. It removes the inhibitions of being incorrect or the fear of risk with musical decisions. Free-form expression will always be correct unless the teacher imposes some form of restriction or expectation. The musical statements are a result of and supported by the knowledge and skill experience of the individual.

The following sequence of events will guide a student (with success) in their first attempts with their own free form melodies.

1. Ask the student to play a slow melody like a lullaby or beautiful ballad. Do not indicate any note, key, tempo, or other musical descriptor. Encourage the student to be free with their melody.
2. Begin the melody on any comfortable pitch and "make up" a melody (lullaby/ballad), experimenting with different notes and rhythms. Do not specify notes or rhythm patterns.
3. Encourage students to play slowly with few notes while listening to the notes moving in different directions to form musical statements.
4. Recognize that the longer (seconds and minutes) the student plays, the more the musical song improves. Listening becomes increasingly focused and directed to melody, note direction, and sound. Notes begin to form meaningful musical patterns and phrases. The feeling of key/tonality develops as the student experiments with accidentals and notes resolve naturally.
5. As the student becomes comfortable playing simple melodies (usually after three to five practice sessions), suggest playing a melody that will reflect the following styles.

    *A happy spirited melody*
    *Sad, somber song, as in losing a friend*
    *Ethnic dance style (Spanish, Mexican, Latin, etc.)*
    *As an eagle soaring through the mountains*
    *Running away (rapid, fleeting, swirl of notes)*
    *A march in the style of John Philip Sousa*
    *A melody in the style of Mozart, Bach, or other composer*

**Finale**

The outlined procedures for free-form expression are perhaps one of the most important musical experiences for your students. Early in my career, I was discouraged with how students responded to phrases and musical expression. After reading many textbooks, I found that musical expression cannot be programmed, as was so often the case. As a professional clarinetist, I found the results were too mechanical without any connection to the feeling of a phrase. This mystery of what was correct when feeling music too often resulted as being contrived expression. Thus, came "free-form expression" which immediately eliminated many barriers my students experienced when trying to play with more feeling. Their musically expressive phrases changed dramatically . . . we were finally making beautiful music! The mystery no longer existed; the feeling or connection was made between composer, conductor, performer, and audience.

With this recipe I encourage you to jump the hurdles of notation, and bring a new world of music making to your students. I assure you the results will be musically rewarding.

*Any sounds in any combination and in any succession are henceforth free to be used in a musical continuity.* — Claude Debussy ➖●

# Meet the Composer: The Next Best Thing to Actually Being There

*Mitchell Lutch*

Music educators must often work within budgetary constraints, which limit the possibility for face-to-face student/composer interaction. With the teacher's thorough rehearsal planning, ensemble members can still reap great benefits from interaction with composers, using a speakerphone.

**INGREDIENTS:**
Four weeks of conference preparation time, background research from at least three publications on the composer's life and works, contact with the composer, student derived questions, and a speakerphone.

**SERVES:**
All performing student musicians.

- First, select one work by a living composer that your group will be preparing for an upcoming concert.
- Second, upon contacting the composer, propose the teleconference idea. Composers have good reason to respond enthusiastically to a proposed teleconference as it offers them a direct connection to young musicians who could become their strongest advocates.
- Next, after discussing the question and answer format with the composer, ask if he or she would agree to offer feedback to your ensemble's live performance of the particular work. The increased motivation level, precision, and musicality of your ensemble will amply compensate for any low-fidelity signal through the speakerphone. Once the teleconference date has been set, supply your students with background information about the composer as well as the origin and form of the piece. Have them gather questions for the composer that arise while studying the work.
- Establish a firm deadline with your students one week prior to the teleconference date for submitting questions for your review.

Sample questions:

- How do you decide on the form when writing a particular composition?
- Which comes first, the medium or the musical idea?
- Is there a mindset or approach you would want to communicate to conductors and/or players when they rehearse and perform your music?
- To what extent do you take into account pleasing the players or audience when composing?

- Do you ever conduct your own compositions and, if so, how has it influenced your composing?
- How do you start composing a particular work? What inspires you? Do you start with a melody, and then add the accompaniment?
- How do you go about getting your music published?
- What advice do you have for high school students who would like to start composing?
- What advice do you have for young composers who would like to gain rehearsal and performance opportunities for their works?

Two teleconference examples:

- Don Freund, Professor of Music, Indiana University at Bloomington. *Jug Blues and Flat Pickin'* (MMB Music, rental). This student/composer interaction included discussion of the work's formal structure and raised the students' awareness of the importance of attending to detail when interpreting notation and the potential distortion of the composer's intent that can occur when such details are overlooked.
- Our performance of Samuel Adler's *American Duo* (Boosey & Hawkes) took place in March 2002. In recognition of Music in Our Schools Month an intriguing addition to the usual performances of prepared repertoire was added to the evening's concert. Students and teachers gave brief demonstrations of notable classroom teaching and learning approaches. Our concert band not only performed an engaging rendition of the work, but also presented a prerecorded message to the audience from the composer himself, an outgrowth of our inspiring teleconference. Mr. Alder responded enthusiastically to our original proposal for a live speakerphone address to the audience, but regretfully was unable to, due to a scheduling conflict. The novel idea of a prerecorded message, suggested by a student, proved to be resoundingly successful. It riveted the audience's attention to the words of a passionate creative artist who had made an indelible impression on our young musicians, elevating their awareness of music as a unique art form. Mr. Adler's prerecorded comments for those in attendance at that evening's concert were as follows:

> I want to tell you how excited I am that young people such as you are taking up the mantle for this kind of music. After all, a composer can only speak through others and we are so happy that young people are excited about playing our music. I know that my teacher, Aaron Copland, whose influence pervades this piece, was always so anxious to go to young people and converse with them because you are the future. I want to say to the parents and administrators that the only way our culture is going to succeed and grow in our country is by encouraging these young people to play, do their utmost, and to get a new spiritual experience which music can give. Mendelssohn was once asked what music does? He said, "Music can say those things that are too precious to put into words." I feel we can communicate best through music because we can express our deepest selves. I thank you for all of your efforts. Keep on doing it because you will create better lives through music. —Samuel Adler, March 26, 2002

The educational benefits of the teleconference are far reaching and only a phone call away. ➤

# Listening Critically

*Matthew McInturf*

Critical listening is the foundation for developing musicianship. The principles of critical listening apply to both individual and ensemble skills.

**INGREDIENTS:**
Basic exercises for instrumentalists at every stage of development. Examples would include long tones, scales, Remington studies, chorale studies, and articulation exercises.

**SERVES:**
Instrumental students and ensembles.

Critical listening is primarily an intellectual exercise. Everyone in the room hears the same sound in a physical/acoustic sense. The difference is how the individual interprets what is heard. The important part of teaching young instrumentalists to listen critically is to understand what they are hearing and guide them to a more mature musical understanding. Rather than teaching students to react to specific instructions, we're trying to teach them to compare their personal performance to a mature musical standard. This is most important at the very beginning stages, where they develop habits that will determine their progress for many years to come.

Before we can teach students to listen, it is crucial that we define what we want the student to hear. In order to seek excellence, we should look to professional models to determine how students should sound. This does not mean that every student will instantly perform like an orchestral musician, but that we should have high expectations for student skills. Too often, teachers accept less than excellent performance because the students are young, and that is what they are accustomed to hearing from young students. In that case, the students are essentially defining the criteria for performance, instead of the teacher. If we seek professional models of performance, we can commend and encourage our students without limiting their aspirations.

Engaging the student in critical listening also helps students to apply general principles in a way that is appropriate for them as individuals. There are certain principles that are true for all wind instruments, but do not necessarily take into account an individual's facial structure or the character of a particular instrument. For example, an oboist uses air very differently than a tubist. Students who have an accurate idea of the result they should be achieving can be more directly engaged in solving their own playing problems.

Ultimately, teaching students to listen critically transforms the classroom into a partnership between the student and the teacher. In effect, everyone has the same goal. It is, of course, essential to provide accurate information about playing the instrument. However, this can become a one-sided conversation when the student performs and is told by the teacher what to do next. A simple prescriptive instruction presumes, perhaps incorrectly, that the student understands what the teacher is listening for in the student's performance. Unless teachers engage students in determining what performance outcome they should expect, this is very unlikely.

There are two major strategies for engaging the student in the listening process: questioning and singing. Using these strategies, the teacher can begin to determine what the student hears. There can be almost infinite variations on questions or exercises to be sung, but we should think in terms of reaching basic performing goals first.

Questions should be prioritized in terms of sound quality, pitch, and articulation. Appropriate questions for evaluating how a student perceives their sound would include these examples:

- Is your sound clear?
- Do you hear anything in your sound beside tone?
- Does it sound easy and effortless?
- Does it feel easy to do?
- Does it ring?

Performing or playing recordings of professional musicians is an excellent way of helping students to define these concepts and compare their personal results. Similar questions can be developed for pitch and articulation. Pitch questions should focus on stability in the beginning. Is the pitch steady, or does it change? Articulations can be compared to shapes. Is there a bump at the beginning of the note?

For students to effectively self-evaluate their achievements, the teacher must refine their understanding of their musical goal. Singing is used to determine how well defined the student's concept has become. Having the student sing a pitch will tell the teacher if the student is listening for the correct pitch. Similarly, the student can model articulations. At any point, the teacher can address the student's understanding and have them sing again. The crucial factor is making sure that the student's understanding is ahead of their performing proficiency. Here, a cautionary word is in order: the student's understanding of their musical goal must stay within achievable limits. If their goal seems overwhelming, they will be frustrated and less motivated. When students can model an appropriate goal for their performance, they will have the ability to collaborate in the process of improving as a musician.

Teaching students to listen critically is a powerful tool that can break the model of the teacher dispensing information and the student implementing it. It enlists students in cooperative learning and gives them evaluative tools that will create more opportunities for success. It also gives teachers a method of instilling higher standards and motivating students on a musical level. ➤●

# Conducting in Music, Not Just in Time

*Allan McMurray*

The movement of the conductor is an important part of the rehearsal as well as the performance. But many conductors limit their movement to the redundancy of time keeping and beat patterns. This means that only stopping and talking, and not watching the conductor, encourages expressive playing.

**INGREDIENTS:**
A quality piece of music that is dance-like or contains sustained tempo within the technical "comfort zone" of the ensemble. Thorough knowledge of the score by the teacher, which includes decisions on phrasing, mood, and style.

**SERVES:**
All conductors and musicians.

Looking like a beat pattern is not looking like the music any more than looking like a foot is looking like a complete person. When describing a beautiful or exciting piece of music, the time signature is rarely mentioned. It is the mood, the feeling, and the style, the *effect* of a piece that is the most important consideration of the beauty of any meaningful piece of music. And it is those aspects that the conductor must visually represent and reinforce to the ensemble. The best conductors seek to nonverbally communicate to the ensemble individually and collectively. Included in this communication is setting tempo in motion, phrase shape, dynamic interpretations, destinations, balance, tone color, note shape, releases (entry to silence), and empathy with the expressive intent of the piece.

To eliminate excessive time-beating, the conductor must lead by empowering not by controlling. The conductor must encourage the ensemble to listen for the internal pulse and then must give the ensemble the responsibility to sustain it without time-beating or a metronome. The conductor needs to monitor this "internal pulse" and only intercede when someone speeds up or slows down. By recognizing the students who are doing the best at this, leaders can be identified and other students can be directed to listen to those players/singers and match them. It is no different than a jazz ensemble listening to a rhythm section. The students use their ears to hear the pulse rather than their eyes to see it.

It is both the conductor's and the student's responsibility to listen and evaluate, to interact with the moment, to compare the ideal with reality. If needed, a single gesture or a few beats directed with eye contact can bring the ensemble back to its internal pulse. Once the ensemble has learned to maintain the tempo initiated by the conductor, the conductor is free from needing to conduct every beat and every meter. This can be included in any warm-up or piece of music or section of music that has a steady pulse. Any changes in pulse, rubato, fermatas, etc., can still be initiated by the conductor, but usually with smaller gestures because the absence of redundancy makes each gesture used seem more important. Cueing entrances with eye contact and a left-hand gesture is effortless, indicating dynamic changes can be smooth and extended over the entire life of a crescendo or diminuendo without "speed bumps." The expressive gesture then becomes the expectation of nonverbal communication and every student becomes a better listener in the process. ➡●

# Song and Dance: It's All About Articulation

*Charlie Menghini*

Performing music in an appropriate style requires that all musicians understand and execute notated articulations with the correct emphasis. Understanding the type of music to be performed and following these simple guidelines will give your instrumentalist(s) a great start!

**INGREDIENTS:**
A whiteboard (chalkboard), two basic concepts, and continued application and reinforcement of information until it becomes a habit.

**SERVES:**
All wind (and percussion) students.

On the board, draw a big whole note. Immediately underneath the whole note, write the word "TAH" so the "T" is under the left edge of the whole note, the "A" is under the center of the whole note, and the "H" is under the right edge of the whole note.

There are two basic concepts that we must understand and apply. First, is that each note has three parts: the start, the sustain, and the release. On a wind instrument, the start of the note is usually a consonant. There are two types of consonants, hard consonants and soft consonants. When articulating most music, players usually use a hard consonant such as the letter *t* or *d*. This is strictly a tongue motion and there is no air or breath support involved in making this tongue movement. Have students practice saying *t* repeatedly and *d* repeatedly. Avoid having them say *tee* or *taa*. Emphasize that this is only a tongue movement and involves no air.

The sustain portion of the note is created by a vowel. Air. Vowels are the letters: *a, e, i, o,* and *u*. Create vowel sounds by engaging the stomach muscles (diaphragm), opening the mouth, and releasing the air. The tongue does not move. Direct your students to sustain the vowel sounds *a* and *e*. Next, have your students sustain the *a* vowel and open the mouth to create an *ah* sound. Do the same with the *e* vowel.

The release part of the note is usually the letter *h*. It is a motion of relaxation. It is the same action as if they were "fogging up" glass. Have your students form their mouths to the letter *h* several times.

When combining the start (consonant), sustain (vowel), and release (relaxation) in an organized and timely manner, we execute an articulation. Have your students say the word *tah*, paying particular attention to all three parts of the note, the start, the sustain, and the release. Shorter notes spend less time on the sustain (vowel) and longer notes spend more time on the sustain (vowel). Whereas the articulation for an eighth note may be *tah,* the articulation for a quarter note might look like *taah* and the whole note might be best represented by *taaaaaaaah.*

Our second concept deals with the two types of music, song and dance. Song music is lyrical in nature. Song music requires air, and the emphasis should be placed on the "sustain" of the note. When students perform a lyrical passage, the emphasis must remain on the vowel or sustain of the note, and they should be instructed to keep the vowel sound constant even when using a legato tongue. Tongue "over the air stream" is one way to express this concept. Of course when slurring a passage, the tongue begins the line and the air continues throughout. It is important that students remember to keep the stomach muscles (diaphragm) engaged throughout the entire musical phrase.

Dance music is rhythmic in nature. Dance music requires a good start to the note and the emphasis should be placed on the start of the note. Heavier dance music requires a heavier, more marcato attack. Lighter dance music requires the player to move faster through the start and sustain of the note and place more emphasis on the release, the *h* part of the articulation.

The next time you are performing a piece of music, determine whether it is a song or a dance. If it is a song, instruct your musicians to emphasize the vowel throughout the note. If a dance, instruct them to place more emphasis on the start of the note or use a stronger consonant, with a good firm tongue stroke.

To help apply these concepts to our percussionists, think of mallet/stick selection. For song music you may want to select a softer mallet or a stick with a wooden tip. Softer mallets tend to flatten a bit as they strike the drum head or bar, thus dispersing the energy over a larger area, allowing the lower overtones to ring and providing for a softer attack. In dance music the opposite will be true. A harder mallet or stick with a nylon tip will not spread and will displace its energy in a smaller area, thus enhancing the higher overtones, resulting in a brighter, more percussive attack. ━●

# Preparing for a Successful Adjudicated Performance

*Stephen W. Miles*

Assessment is a vital component of any worthwhile academic endeavor. It provides a method for determining if we have met certain established standards of achievement. With performance ensembles, it tells us if we have met the goal of presenting a musical performance that reflects the intent of the composer. While every director strives to achieve excellence in their ensemble performance, why is it that so many adjudicated programs do not meet the criteria we associate with excellence? How do we go about improving the likelihood of achieving a successful adjudicated performance? The following recipe outlines a variety of ideas and strategies designed to help achieve a technically competent and musically satisfying performance in an adjudicated setting.

## INGREDIENTS:

A balanced and carefully chosen program is perhaps the single most important element contributing to a successful adjudicated performance. The music should not only be of high quality and musical value, but it must also have depth and substance and must wear well with the students over the extended period of preparation. Consider reading through lots of music during the selection process and seeking the input of the students—understanding that quality literature may not immediately captivate, but will grow on them with time and study. Also, be sure that all students have something interesting to play, especially considering the amount of time they will most likely be spending on these selections.

Another critical ingredient in repertoire selection is how well the music fits the ensemble. When looking at the suitability of repertoire, consider the technical skill, musical maturity and instrumentation of the ensemble. Make certain that all musical elements (chord tones, soloists, percussion voices, etc.) are covered. Not enough horns in your band? Rewrite the parts for alto sax, low trumpet, low clarinet, or baritone. The important consideration is that all of the notes are played and that the "revision" comes as close to staying with the composer's intent as possible.

## SERVES:

All instrumental ensemble members.

## Preparation

Many musical and pedagogical issues must be addressed in the preparation of a successful adjudicated performance. For the purpose of this recipe, we will look at five areas, including fundamentals, tools and strategies, podium issues (how do you impact the rehearsal?), musicality issues, and what to do (or not do) on the day of the performance.

*Fundamentals*

In every rehearsal, fundamental concepts and skills such as breath control, posture, hand position, bowing, articulation, and counting must be targeted and reinforced. Consider using a method book or system of addressing these fundamentals and engage all of the musicians—percussionists included—everyday. Don't neglect this area and focus only on the adjudicated repertoire. Invest in the students' musical and technical growth—not just rote teaching of the performance literature.

*Tools and Strategies*

The following ideas, presented in no particular order, have been used with great success by many ensemble directors. (The application of specific strategies will necessarily be based on the needs of the particular situation.) Sing some every day, especially during warm-up and tuning. Use an electronic tuner to establish a pitch center, and use it as a reference during the rehearsal. Take some time each class to train the students to listen and adjust. Remind them that there are basically three options when tuning—the note is either flat, sharp, or in tune. When in doubt—do something. If that something makes it worse, then reverse the action.

Use tuning charts so every student learns their pitch tendencies on every note in their practical playing range. Be sure the warm-up has relevance to the music being studied for performance. Vary the tempo when playing scales so the students get used to watching. Simply telling students to watch almost never works. Watching and responding to the conductor is a learned skill that is critical to success in performance. Work on fundamentals such as rhythm every day. Develop a rehearsal and performance rubric for self and peer evaluation. Record your rehearsals (both audio and video), copy adjudication sheets (with the rubrics), and have the students listen to or watch and assess their performance. Hold each student accountable for being able to play all of his or her music accurately. Use an audiotape if necessary. Listen to every student and grade his or her performance.

Teach phrasing from day one—how to start, when to break, how to end. Identify and point out similarities and contrasts. Break down difficult sections so that the components can be isolated and clarified. Slow . . . it . . . down. If you must leave a section before it is fixed, make sure that the students don't assume that they have it right just because you moved on. Invite colleagues, other school directors, or college directors to come in and listen to or work with your group. It can be very useful for students to hear similar feedback from another source. It can also provide a fresh perspective for you as well.

## Podium Issues (Or: How Are You, the Director, Impacting the Rehearsal/ Performance?)

Be sure you have a concept of how the pieces should sound. (Now more than ever there are quality recordings of most ensemble literature. They can be extremely valuable when used wisely.) Read the score, be careful and clear with tempi, and make sure that tempi and dynamic proportions are in order. Is your baton technique clear, readable, expressive, and in time? Practice in front of a mirror and ask "Is this what I want my students to see?" Are you helping or getting in the way? Video tape yourself conducting a rehearsal; you may be surprised by what you see and hear.

Stress musicality from the outset, not just after the notes are there. Listen when the ensemble plays. (Don't sing along and cover the errors you need to hear and subsequently fix.) Have you made sure to cover all chord tones if your instrumentation is not complete? Rescore the parts if necessary. Remember, there is never an acceptable reason for chord tones or melody lines to be missing. Wrong notes are also never acceptable. Have you checked *every* note in *every* measure of *every* part? Unlike most academic areas, 90 percent accuracy in music performance does not earn an A.)

### Musicality Issues

When addressing musicality—and we should always be addressing musicality— ask yourself the following questions: Is the ensemble playing with good tone quality and control? Is the ensemble playing in tune? Is the ensemble balanced? (Think McBeth.) Are all of the rhythms being performed accurately and in time? Is there a sense of ensemble precision? (Is it "tight"—in a good way?) Are all of the notes being played? Can the ensemble handle the technical demands of the music? Is the playing expressive? Are the phrases shaped and are the lines going somewhere? Are repeated notes given direction? Are phrase endings tapered? Is the last note of the phrase a chord and can all of the voices be heard?

### The Day of the Performance

Be sure you handle the warm-up at the festival the same way you handle it everyday. (Now is not the time to experiment.) Don't go over solo sections—a missed note here can really shake a young player's confidence and composure. Remember that a big part of the warm-up process before the performance is getting the students mentally ready to perform. You want them to be focused, yet relaxed and ready to play their best.

### Parting Thoughts

As directors of student ensembles, we are the single most powerful factor influencing the musical experience that our students have in the ensemble setting. Choose music wisely, work fundamentals every day, stress musicality, set high standards, and hold the students accountable for meeting those expectations. Remember that if we achieve our goal of presenting a musical performance reflecting the composer's intent, we will not only have achieved success with the performance itself, but we will also have facilitated significant student learning in the process.

Although the recipe for achieving success in an adjudicated performance is a very complex one involving many carefully selected and blended ingredients, when it is thoughtfully prepared and presented, the results can be most satisfying. *Bon appetit!* ➤

# Empower Your Students to Fine-Tune Your Ensemble

*Linda R. Moorhouse*

Intonation, or accuracy of pitch and pitch matching, is a multi-pronged process that includes (1) good fundamental tone, (2) knowledge of the idiosyncrasies of the instrument (e.g., 5th partial on brass instruments is flat, upper register of saxophone is sharp to the lower register, throat tones on clarinets are sharp, etc.) (3) knowledge of the individual pitch tendencies of each note on the instrument, (4) knowledge of how intervals relate to one another, and (5) the ability to blend tone and match pitch with others.

**INGREDIENTS:**
Instruments in good working order, staff paper, pencils, fingering charts, classroom or individual tuner, patience, and persistence.

**SERVES:**
All instrumental students.

Have you ever felt sorry for the director who has every instrument on stage "pushing and pulling" slides and joints to match the concert B-flat tuning note before the band begins to play? (And this is after an adequate warm-up somewhere else!) How confident are you about your students' knowledge of their horns and their ability to play "in tune?" Some students can play on the same instrument for years at a time and not know the idiosyncrasies of their horn. Teaching the young musician how to recognize and produce good tone is the first objective. Teaching the student how to master their instrument so they can play it in tune and match pitch with others is the next step—skills that can be acquired with patience, practice, and time.

In the last few years, the availability of personal tuners has increased considerably. Although checking isolated notes with tuners in rehearsal can be helpful in some situations, training students to use them to learn about their individual instruments may be a better use of the device—a process best done outside of rehearsal or in sectionals.

Students should begin with a good working knowledge of their instrument—not just fingerings, but how the instrument operates (e.g., overtone series, recommended factory settings for valve and tuning slides and/or joints of each instrument, French horn right-hand placement, and how the "pushing and pulling" of any part of the instruments affects the tuning of the instrument, etc.). Once the horn is "factory set," the tuner can help identify any individual and/or register pitch discrepancies.

## The Tuning Test

The objective of the Tuning Test is to examine and record how sharp, flat, or "in tune" each note is throughout the normal practical range of the instrument. Students need blank staff paper (or any special handouts you have created), pencils, and fingering chart showing the full range of their instruments. By using the fingering charts, they can test the pitch of alternate fingerings. Students fill in the proper clef(s) and transfer the full range of notes chromatically onto the staff paper, repeating notes if alternate fingerings are tested. (Include fingering information or valve combinations if alternate fingerings are used to differentiate between regular and alternate fingerings on the same pitch.) Under each note, draw a small line–information is recorded in this space. Students need to know how to decipher the information the tuner provides, as different models vary. Decide on a notation system to use in recording how sharp or flat notes sound. Some tuners are more meticulous and informative than others, especially the larger, more expensive classroom tuners.

After a proper warm-up and brief tuning note, the student taking the test turns away from the tuner to begin. Without looking at the tuner, the student plays each note on their chart at a mezzo forte to forte level for a good five seconds with the administrator (student or teacher) recording the pitch characteristics of each. The administrator records how sharp, flat, or "in tune" each note is, without helping the test-taker or giving commentary. The student taking the test aims to "stop the dial" on each note. While younger students may only be able to play a limited range of notes, encourage older students to test the full practical range of their instruments as soon as possible, without vibrato.

Instruments are affected by four major conditions: (1) variations in loudness and softness, (2) changing temperatures, (3) insufficient warm-up, and (4) playing off the tuning standard (if the "standard" is A = 440). It is an interesting insight for students to take a portion of the test when instruments are properly warmed up, and when the instruments are cold. Taking the test with and without mutes is a "must" for brass players, and taking the test at various dynamic levels is another valuable resource tool for all students.

Once finished, switch and have the administrator (if applicable) go through the same procedure after a proper warm-up period. You can pair any combination of instruments, or test any number of students. It will take about fifteen to twenty minutes per person to take the test. Once finished, students make a copy of their chart to study, and turn the original in for grading and record keeping. Administer the test again after four to six weeks, every grading period, or as needed until students are able to play their horns in tune. Listening skills will improve and students will learn how their instruments should be assembled for the most accurate overall pitch, and more importantly, which notes and/or registers need a critical ear for slight adjustments. Students who possess the best fundamental tones will most likely have the least amount of pitch discrepancies. Also, you will find a correlation between pitch inconsistencies and the different types and/or quality of instruments. Below is a sample of what a partial chart of a Tuning Test might look like.

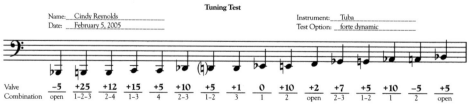

90

If you watch professional musicians before a concert, they will rarely make overt adjustments to their horns while tuning. They know their horns, and they know how to match pitch. Once your students know how to assemble their instruments for optimum tuning, they should be encouraged to make only the slightest adjustments as needed.

Empower your students to master their instruments and to be critical listeners. This will help foster an environment for independent thinking and troubleshooting. And, whether your group plays "in tune" or "out of tune," here's hoping you can do it together! ➤●

# A Recipe for Cymbal Success

*Willis M. Rapp*

Without doubt, the tone quality of cymbals can make or break the music. We can work to develop beautiful wind band sonority with attention to balance, blend, dynamics, and phrasing. And, we can pay careful attention to control of pitch and articulation. However, if we neglect to consider the importance of cymbal sounds, then we fall short of being an advocate for both the music and the composer.

**INGREDIENTS:**
At least one pair of hand cymbals suitable for use with an orchestra or wind band. Select a pair of cymbals with a wide range of overtones. Cymbals that are hand-hammered tend to have a profile that is flatter than cymbals that are only turned on a lathe and not hammered. Avoid the use of marching band cymbals, which tend to have a bright, penetrating sound. An additional ingredient would be a thinner, suspended cymbal of the same size as the hand cymbals. We'll talk about how to use this ingredient later.

**SERVES:**
Every musician, conductor, and audience member when used correctly.

It is interesting to observe the high level of accomplishment by many string, wind, and brass sections that have percussionists in their ensembles who don't seem to know very much about playing cymbals. It is also interesting to note that many student percussionists are not aware of the variety of sounds that can be produced by hand cymbals. Frederick Fennell was quoted as saying, "Cymbals are our most misunderstood, poorly played, and ceremoniously destroyed musical objects." With that in mind, it is time to serve up hand cymbal sounds that are on the same level as the finest sounds produced by today's performing ensembles.

There are many schools of thought when it comes to playing hand cymbals. And, if over-analyzed, it can lead to a situation that is more difficult to improve than a bad golf swing. Clearly, a model is needed. While many are currently available, one of the great masters of this instrument was Benjamin Podemski, cymbalist of the Philadelphia Orchestra in the late 1940s. He shared his technique and approach with young Fred Hinger, who joined the orchestra in 1948. While Hinger became principal timpanist in 1951, he generously shared Podemski's approach to cymbals with those of us who were fortunate enough to study with him. The following was Podemski's approach to producing legato strokes on hand cymbals, as first taught to me in 1971 by Fred D. Hinger. This is the technique that Podemski used to play some of the most glorious crashes in the orchestral repertoire.

**The Podemski Appproach**

*Presented Here for a Right-Handed Performer*
- Take the heavier cymbal in the left hand.
- The right hand holds the lighter cymbal on top.
- Feet should be shoulder-width apart for balance.
- The cymbals should be positioned at a slight angle, with the top edges toward the performer's left side.

*Learning the Legato Cymbal Crash*
- Practice a right-hand motion similar to a down stroke in drumming, which will initially allow the right cymbal to "drop" onto the left cymbal. This practice motion will sound similar to a loud hi-hat sound, and you will have to reset the right hand each time you perform this practice stroke.
- The complete motion allows the hands to be set for the next stroke.
- Finally, the full stroke motion is used again, this time with Podemski's legato technique of allowing the top edges of the plates to remain together just slightly before the right hand returns to the "up" position. This will produce a sound with a bit of a "sizzle" in it (to your ears). This "sizzle" is the action of the two plates continuing to vibrate against each other, and allows one to produce a longer sound.
- The longer the note value, the more time the top edges should spend together after the initial "drop" of the full stroke. For a fortissimo cymbal crash with maximum resonance and sustain, a complete follow-through of this stroke will allow the individual cymbals to move into a position where they hang parallel with the floor.
- As you become more comfortable with the legato technique, you will begin to notice an interaction between the two hands; in fact, the best sounds are produced when there is motion in both hands. The full stroke action of the right hand is now complimented with a similar action from underneath in the left hand. While this is more of an advanced technique, perhaps exceeding our recipe for simple/cymbal success, you will certainly notice a big difference in the tone quality of cymbal crashes using the slower legato motion approach.

**Some Additional Condiments**
- Cymbalists should recognize that short "down" strokes sound one way, and short "up" strokes sound different. Often times, a careful combination of these short down and up strokes brings a fresh interpretation to a passage.
- The softest of notes can be managed on hand cymbals with full plate contact. Hold the cymbals horizontally, and while maintaining contact with the top edges of the plates, just slightly lift the bottom edges of the plates as you produce the pianissimo note.
- Using a thinner suspended cymbal of the same size allows you to fashion an even lighter set of hand cymbals for special effects.

Experiment, refine these techniques, and serve! ➤

# Solving Technical and Musical Problems in Rehearsals: An Upside-Down Cake

*Jeffrey Renshaw*

**INGREDIENTS:**

The most important ingredient is musicianship. Combine this with an equal amount of understanding of the music being performed. Add a cup of imagination. Mix well and pour into a very productive rehearsal.

**SERVES:**

All instrumental and vocal ensembles.

Problem solving is arguably the priority of most rehearsals. Problems range from assisting individuals with their parts to combining parts into a meaningful musical whole. Often, we as conductors and performers get caught up in minutia of these problems and literally get in our own way. One of the most effective ways to approach these challenges is to change the parameter.

Many technical challenges can be rethought by approaching them from a musical point of view. Running sixteenth-note passages can easily become a challenge of articulation, tempo consistency, and meter. By approaching the passage in a musical perspective, many of the "hard" parts instantly become easier and they make musical sense because our concentration is on a different parameter. Instead of the "technical" grouping of 1234, 1234, try grouping them within the phrase—1,2341,234.

Another example would be dealing with wide and often awkward note skips. The solution is often in the position within the contour of the phrase or the position of the climax note and how the line builds into it.

Turn the cake over. Musical challenges are often revealed by focusing of technical solutions. These can be rhythmic interpretation, articulation emphasis, or intonation tendencies.

Obviously the longer we "cook" the score in our mind, the more natural the solutions become. Anyone can combine the ingredients of a recipe. Only the master chef knows the secret of how each ingredient interacts with others to create exactly the right taste, consistency, and color of the final product. We must remind ourselves that we deal with an art form, not a microwave entree. ➙

# Developing "H.O.T.S." During Lessons and Rehearsals

*Nathalie Robinson*

*Higher-Order-Thinking-Skills,* or H.O.T.S., are thought processes that enable students to think critically and creatively within a musical context. Improvising, composing, analyzing, and critiquing are pedagogical strategies that facilitate students developing these types of thinking (Bloom, 1956). Students with H.O.T.S. tend to listen analytically, utilize and apply knowledge more readily in new situations, (e.g., long-term learning), and develop a high degree of musical sensitivity.

**INGREDIENTS:**
Tape recorder, playback system, and your own creative juices.

**SERVES:**
All instrumental and vocal students.

We all agree that "drill-and-skill" is necessary for preparing our young performing musicians, but it is not enough. So often we think we have taught a new rhythm, fingering, or scale, only to realize that our students have forgotten it a week later. Students need opportunities to *apply* what they are learning. Personal application is the vehicle through which students gain a more in-depth understanding of the material being presented. For examples, when teaching a new scale during instrumental lessons, ask the students to compose a short composition in that tonality as part of their homework assignment. Set the parameters and pose a musical problem for them to solve: "Using the key of A major, compose an eight-measure piece that captures your feelings about spring."

Choral directors who are teaching sight-singing might ask their students to compose a four-measure warm-up in a specific meter that utilizes the rhythmic patterns and pitch intervals they are studying. These assignments require students to dissect what is being taught and use it in a new context to generate their own musical ideas. In addition to the time spent preparing weekly exercises, students will engage in extramusical thought and energy to create their compositions and prepare them for performance during their next lesson or rehearsal.

Performance of student compositions is essential! Performance provides the catalyst for students to understand that music is an expressive performing art and also sets the stage for personal or small group analysis and critique. Record student performances and provide time for listening. You can guide their listening with questions such as the following:

- What did you think was effective in this composition?
- If you had the opportunity to revise your composition, would you change anything?
- In what ways were the compositions similar and/or different from each other?

The choral director might use the student compositions as sight-singing exercises at the beginning of the rehearsal by putting a few each day on an overhead transparency. Pose the following questions to your students: "Compare these two compositions. Which one did you find more difficult to sing?" and "Why do you think this is so?" Students will be quick to identify that steps are easier to sing than skips, beginning and ending on the tonic provides a feeling of completeness, and repeated or sequenced material is less complicated to sight-read.

Recording and listening to your students' compositions and verbal analyses of their work provides an ideal opportunity for assessment. Students will not only engage in self-assessment, but you will quickly recognize whether or not they understand the musical concepts you were presenting during your lesson. Providing time for listening and discussion builds a foundation that will help guide students' future musical thoughts and decisions as they learn from their own experiences and reflect on their peer's work.

Developing thoughtful young musicians is a goal to which we all aspire. Composition and analysis are the ideal musical tools that enable students to develop their higher-order-thinking-skills. ➤

Bloom, B.S. (1956). *Taxonomy of educational objectives: Handbook 1. Cognitive domain.* New York: David McKay.

# Enhanced Ensemble Sonority via Vowel Modulation

*Timothy Salzman*

A sonorous, balanced, and resonant ensemble sound is the result of a uniform approach to tone production. This approach relies on excellent posture, an adequate air supply, and an oral openness similar to that achieved by great opera singers. Despite the best of intentions, wind players simply cannot produce dark tone with a highly constricted inner oral cavity. The purpose of this recipe is to address that problem in an ensemble setting.

**INGREDIENTS:**
Overhead projector (whiteboard). Dry erase markers. Thoughtful, adjectival tonal descriptions. Teacher-modeled physical, visceral demonstrations. Selected correct and incorrect vowel modulation trials, which are ultimately incorporated into breathing exercises. Strong dose of metaphor or analogy.

**SERVES:**
Brass and woodwind players.

Today's students are immersed in a popular music culture, in which a sense of open, resonant tonality is not modeled. The physicality of their approach to their respective instruments is more visceral/muscular and is based upon visual imagery born of memorized images of MTV guitarists and drummers "windmilling" at their instruments with a rather determined sense of semi-violence. This visceral approach to music making has produced a generation of wind instrumentalists who play with an orally constricted physicality that, at the very least, results in a lack of blend. More predictably the ensemble will adopt a strident tonality that is typically sharp in pitch. This inner oral constriction is difficult to externally perceive. However, this common dilemma can be remedied through rehearsal discussion of the concept of vowel modulation and a subsequent application of a few simple exercises.

Begin with an explanation of what is meant by the inner oral cavity (hereafter referred to by its acronym, IOC). It is helpful to draw a simple, graphic view of a representation of the IOC, a sort of side view X-ray, on an overhead projector or whiteboard/chalkboard (fig. 1).

Figure 1

In a tonally supportive IOC, maximum resonance is achieved by maintaining sufficient space between the teeth (fig. 2a), having a high soft palate (fig. 2b), and a depressed tongue (fig. 2c). However, most students will find these specific physical instructions impossible to apply during the course of playing a particular passage due to "input overload." Instead of burdening the players with unnecessary information regarding the anatomical particulars, which will most often result in a sort of musical "paralysis" on the part of the performer, focus on the notion of vowel modulation, an instruction more easily managed due to the similarities between singing and wind instrument playing.

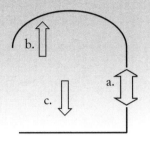

Figure 2

Ask the students to play a concert F while formulating their mouths as if they were going to say *ee*. For this initial sound, a vivid instructional analogy is to ask them to play as if their jaws had been wired shut after a serious accident. Through the course of the held pitch, ask them to modulate the vowel from *ee* through *ah*, *awe*, and finally, to *oh*. Ask them to watch your hands carefully. Initiate the pitch from the podium with each hand closed, thumbs pressed against fingers. While they are playing, open your hands gradually as you "mouth" the various vowels, ultimately stopping on the most open shape, as though you are holding a softball, a profile similar to the drawing above. Repeat the sequence, asking the students to really listen for purposes of evaluating the difference in both tone and pitch during the sequence. They will most probably notice a gradual darkening of tone that is typically accompanied by a lowering in pitch.

It is assumed that posture and an adequate air supply are in place when addressing the IOC issue. An additional and obvious benefit to an open IOC is increased intake, and, if the IOC is maintained during exhalation, a warmer sound will result due to increased flow. Students need to feel the difference between "correct" and "incorrect" in order to make the correct choices regarding their vowel formulation during inhalation. Utilizing the vowel sequence indicated above, ask the students to inhale and hold their breath while formulating each vowel sound, beginning with *ee*. (One inhalation/held breath per vowel formulation.) They will notice an improved ability in the volume of the held breath upon utilizing the more open (*oh*) vowel during inhalation. For director/teachers, breathing is most easily "policed" by sound: correct inhalation is silent. Constricted airways (*ee*) coupled with shallow breathing always generate noisy intakes. ➤●

# Deep-Dish Assessment: Sight-Reading in the Rehearsal

*Deborah Sheldon*

One of the best ways to determine music students' abilities is through sight-reading. It is truly an application of all musical skills in a performance setting. It may be the single best indicator of the development of musicianship that we can use with our students.

**INGREDIENTS:**
A consistent helping of sight-reading in the daily rehearsal, three levels of balanced, achievable sight-reading materials, a thoroughly mixed rehearsal plan, a focus on beautiful sound, and a positive approach.

**SERVES:**
Instrumental students of all levels of development.

Sight-reading is a habit that can improve most aspects of performance among young musicians. Unfortunately, many directors poke at it on an irregular basis throughout the year, only to push it hard right before those magic contest days. It's no wonder there is often fear or distain for the activity. When approached with this erratic schedule, one of the only real concepts that are reinforced is performance anxiety! As an expected part of the daily rehearsal, however, its usefulness cannot be understated. Regular sight-reading strengthens all sorts of concepts and engages students in authentic assessment. It is one of the best ways to get students to problem solve in a music setting.

Initially, it might be difficult to relinquish time to sight-reading in your regular rehearsal schedule. It may seem like it detracts from more specific rehearsal goals. But sight-reading is like a cash bank deposit, leaving you a little short as you make the deposit: less cash in your pocket, fewer minutes for performance rehearsal. In time, though, the investment comes back to you; you accrue interest and the student develops greater musical problem solving skills. Musicians trained in sight-reading transfer performance concepts better than without such experience; they become successful independent music makers. Set aside time during each rehearsal for this activity! It should be a daily expectation.

Carefully consider the materials you choose. Method books work well when teaching younger students, etude books are often appropriate, and your own library will have some good materials. Balance the use of band literature with etudes or other resources that will challenge everyone equally. There might be a vast difference between what your flute players must accomplish in certain band selections, for example, compared to your tuba players.

Select this music carefully to ensure an optimal experience for all. Keep the excerpts short, especially when you first introduce the activity. Short excerpts fit easily into the time you allot and give your students a feeling of accomplishment and closure. Lengthy examples can be frustrating. Shorter examples let them concentrate on a few things at a time and raise the probability of success. As students gain more experience, lengthen the examples. They'll be ready for it.

Your material inventory should cover three levels of difficulty. Match the difficulty level with students' sight-reading adeptness. With less experienced musicians, use examples that fall just below their ability level so they can concentrate on sound quality and expression without having to worry too much about notes and rhythms. As they become more experienced with sight-reading, use music that matches their ability level, peppered with music that falls just above. Continue to add a splash of easy ones. Examples at their skill level will fully test their musical abilities and intuitions. Those that are a bit more complex will give you information on where to focus your efforts next. The easier examples continue to reinforce concepts while boosting confidence.

Mix the elements of the rehearsal from time to time. Don't make the mistake of always placing sight-reading at the end of the rehearsal. You risk running out of time, and at the end of the rehearsal students often get fatigued. Use moments in the rehearsal when the student can approach the task with enthusiasm and energy so they remain fully engaged. Besides, a thorough mixing of rehearsal activities from time to time keeps students alert and on their toes.

Finally, maintain a positive approach and help your musicians to set sight-reading goals. Playing with a *beautiful sound* should be at the top of the list, closely followed by *playing musically*. Correct rhythms and notes are encompassed in this, and that is why it is so important to begin a regular sight-reading plan that begins a bit below ability level and gradually increases in difficulty. With a systematic method, your attitude towards sight-reading will be more positive and you'll transmit less anxiety to your students. The outcome? A deep-dish assessment plan that *is* performance! ➖●

# A Quantitative Approach to Ensemble Dynamics

*Thomas E. Slabaugh, II*

As an ensemble director, I am often asking members of my group to readjust their dynamic levels to accommodate the needs of the musical score. This is, in part, due to the vagueness of traditional dynamic markings that originated from the late sixteenth century. While not a new technique, I use an approach that translates the dynamic expression into numerical terms, all the while encouraging ensemble members to listen and evaluate their individual volume, tone color, and ensemble blend.

**INGREDIENTS:**
Voices, instruments, and ears! Begin each rehearsal with this exercise, encouraging student experimentation, while monitoring and reporting on their collective progress. Consistency is essential.

**SERVES:**
All instrumental and voice students.

**Step 1:** Ask all ensemble members to sing or play a unison pitch at the middle of their dynamic ranges, also known as *mf*. Direct them to adjust their volume levels so they are able to hear themselves equally as loud as they are able to hear their fellow ensemble members. Always encourage ensemble members to produce a beautiful tone that is not superimposed on the lowest pitch in the ensemble. Rather, the goal is to sound as if there is only one performer producing a lovely unison sound. Encourage experimentation and adjustment of both volume levels and tone color to achieve the best result. Once a melded and beautiful sound is achieved, ask students to refer to that volume as an ensemble *mf* (e.g., I am able to hear myself equally as loud as I am able to hear my fellow ensemble members).

**Step 2:** Now ask the ensemble members to sing or play a little louder, so they are able to hear themselves a bit more prominently than they are able to hear the other ensemble members. Encourage all ensemble members to produce the most beautiful tone possible and to refrain from superimposing their sound on the lowest pitch in the ensemble. Once a good result has been achieved, ask students to refer to this volume as an ensemble *f*.

**Step 3:** Ask students to produce the same volume as in step 1, also known as an ensemble *mf*. Now, have ensemble members sing or play the same pitch a little softer than *mf*, so that they are able to hear the other members of the ensemble a bit louder than they are able to hear themselves. As always, encourage the ensemble members to produce a beautiful tone that is not superimposed on the lowest pitch in the ensemble. Once the result has been achieved, have ensemble members refer to this volume as *mp*.

**Step 4:** Continue this exercise in a similar fashion until you have established a series of volume levels that ensemble members are able to reference during rehearsals and performances. It is helpful to visually reinforce this concept by producing a diagram that represents dynamic levels as numerically assigned values. For example:

| Dynamic Level | Volume of Self | Volume of Others |
|---|---|---|
| *fff* | 80% | 20% |
| *ff* | 70% | 30% |
| *f* | 60% | 40% |
| *mf* | 50% | 50% |
| *mp* | 40% | 60% |
| *p* | 30% | 70% |
| *pp* | 20% | 80% |
| *ppp* | 10% | 90% |

**Step 5:** Use this diagram to illustrate the dynamic range music is capable of producing without a change in assigned dynamic levels. This is often referred to as "line" in music and can be illustrated in a quantitative fashion as follows:

> The section between rehearsal A and B is marked *f*, but the melody and harmony have a clear shape that grows towards the fifth measure and recedes to the measure before B. Try thinking of the dynamics beginning at rehearsal A as 60/40 percent and growing to 69/31 percent at the peak of phrase in the fifth measure. Allow the music to recede to the original 60/40 percent level at one measure before rehearsal B. Remember, your tone color and blend cannot change during these subtle changes in dynamics.

The result of a quantitative approach to dynamics is an ensemble that is able to easily adjust their volume, balance, and blend to varying performance locations and situations. Further, all ensemble members have a heightened awareness of their musical role through the constant, directed-listening exercise that begins each rehearsal session. ➤

# Strengthening Instrumental Ensemble Tuning with Vocalization and Solfège

*Frederick Speck*

As children, the first medium for expressing our musical imagination is the voice. When people sing, they sense a direct link to tone as physical vibrations in their bodies. Further, when group of musicians sing together, it is apparent that singers make what seems to be an intuitive effort to bring pitch into agreement. With this in mind, employing vocalization as a regular component of instrumental music training is a productive tool for drawing the student to a closer awareness of the intimacy of their own tone production and their relationship to others in the ensemble setting.

**INGREDIENTS:**
**Solfège** is an excellent system for developing an understanding of both diatonic and chromatic sounds in tonal music. Using moveable Do (Do being the first scale degree) in both major and minor, the musician is able to give a discreet name and address to all of the pitches in a tonal context. Hearing within the tonality fosters the development of good intonation as a positive byproduct of accurate expectation.

**SERVES:**
All instrumental and vocal students.

Advantages of using moveable Do solfège include:

1. Solfège syllables provide specific names for all chromatic pitches used in tonal music. Neutral syllables or numbers do not. In addition, when instrumental students use neutral syllables, it tends to become and "outside-in" approach, where the sound of the example played on an instrument directs where the pitch will be sung, rather than developing an acute aural image so that there is a better target of expectation for instrumental pitch placement.
2. Solfège syllables provide better vowels for singing than numbers.
3. Solfège syllables are specific only to pitch relationship, creating no confusion of terms, whereas numbers are often used in counting systems as well.
4. The moveable Do system maintains the same names for Do and Sol polarities in any key, regardless of whether the music is in major or minor.

This system can be presented effectively to students at any age, as there is always at least an elementary level of readiness.

**Directions**

**Melody** alone is used to begin the process, the teacher needing only to sing bits of solfège to the students, asking them to join into the flow of "call and imitation." This "repeat after me" approach makes it an easy access experience for the students, because the teacher goes first, with the students being bolstered by safety in numbers. This should proceed from simple two- or three-note groups, to complete phrases as both the teacher and students gain comfort. Alternate or mix the order of asking the students to either play back or sing back the examples. Through this process, the students develop the listening skill of taking musical dictation as they play back in correct pitches, rhythm, volume, and style. In addition, this exercise requires the musicians to respond to the teacher and to one another, without looking at a page. This automatically focuses the listening. Ultimately, this model can even be developed into structured improvisation.

**Harmonic progressions** can be taught in such a way that the musicians are not dependent on music reading to create them. An obvious benefit to the process is that it calls upon both the memories and aural skills of the performers for achieving success. The basic chord connections for a standard harmonic progression can be taught by introducing two basic chords, then adding more as the musicians demonstrate readiness. The process is simple: have the ensemble perform a chord as a melodic arpeggiation (demonstrate in solfège), then sound it as a chord. The teacher may chose to dictate that a few particular bass voices perform as roots of the chords, but other than that, students should choose freely. A suggested process is tonic and subdominant alternation first (as each chord has Do in common), after which the dominant, then finally the supertonic in first inversion may be added to complete the progression I-IV-ii6/5-V-I. This progression drill is even more valuable in minor. Young students can develop this skill, and all high school students are capable of it within a short period of time — many within two rehearsal warm-up periods.

**Minor-key aural training** provides an intervallic richness, both melodically and harmonically, that is advantageous in instrumental ear training. This premise stems from the point of view that musical structures that exemplify differences are easier for the ear/mind to catalogue, remember, and identify than those that are similar or identical. As a visual analogy, one might consider the ability to identify and name the four crayons red, yellow, blue and white, as compared to the same task with yellow-orange, melon, salmon, and peach.

## Melodic Elements

1. The melodic materials of the harmonic minor scale provide discrete interval contrast in the first three tones of the scale: Do-Re (whole step) and Re-Me (half step). By comparison, the major scale moves through the first three scale degrees Do-Re-Mi via two consecutive whole steps. Consecutive replication of intervals produces aural ambiguity.
2. Though consecutive whole steps are present in the harmonic minor scale in the segment, Me-Fa-Sol, the ambiguity is mitigated, as the point of arrival is Sol, the root of the dominant chord and a pitch of strong tonal polarity.
3. The sixth scale degree of the harmonic minor, Le, is a half step above Sol, having a strong tendency back to Sol, and as such, better fixing Sol in the musician's aural imagery.
4. The seventh scale degree of the harmonic minor, Ti, like its counterpart in major, functions as the leading tone and inflects to the tonic, Do.

In practice, the use of harmonic minor allows the teacher to avert some unfortunate mishaps that often occur as musicians create an inaccurate aural groove through faulty renditions of major-key exercises.

1. Musicians often place the major third too high in both melodic and harmonic contexts. Though the melodic major third is also encountered in minor, it is not found in the common first through third scale degrees, where musicians are likely to inadvertently train themselves to accept a major third that is too sharp.
2. Musicians also often place the fourth scale degree, Fa, too high. This may be a consequence of the inaccurate, widened major seconds that often begin a major scale. A positive approach to teaching the fourth scale degree is by melodic descent from Sol to Fa, just as occurs in the presence of dominant harmony.

### Harmonic Elements

1. The harmonic materials of basic tonal progressions in harmonic minor provide greater differentiation of chord types than the same progressions in major. For instance, I-iv-V-I provides obvious contrast of minor and major, with the only major sound being that of the dominant chord. The same functional progression in major presents only major chords, I-IV-V-I.
2. The differences in the harmonic richness of major and minor are even more apparent in the common progression, i-iv-ii $^{\text{half-dim } 6/5}$-V-I, as there are three distinctive chord sounds present in a context that features the major chord only once, and then in the unique function of the dominant. These chord-type differences provide greater contrast than the major-key version, I-IV-ii$^{6/5}$-V-I, in which major sonorities prevail and saturate the texture with the same chord construction. Such saturation with the same interval constructions tends toward aural ambiguity.

### Mix Well

These processes work well at the beginning of the rehearsal, in that they demand attentiveness and concentration. However, the application of these procedures can yield equally valuable benefits during other parts of the rehearsal when applied to repertoire that is being studied. Intonationally unstable phrases may be alternated between singing and playing, not only by the musicians who have the specific passage, but by everyone in the room. All may first take the basic dictation and then sing it back. At the teacher's discretion, some may sing while others play the passage. All will gain a better concept of the passage and have better aural targets as a result.

Typically, the greater the lyrical and tonal harmonic potential of the work, the more successful the exercise will be. The following are examples of works at varied grade levels that provide excellent materials for using the voice to build an accurate aural imagination: *The Red River Valley*, by Pierre LaPlante; *As Summer Was Just Beginning*, by Larry Daehn; *I'll Be Home A'Fore Ye*, by Julie Giroux; *Ammerland*, by Jacob deHaan; *Salvation Is Created*, by Pavel Tschesnokoff/Bruce Houseknecht; *Prelude No. 2*, by George Gershwin/John Krance; *O Magnum Mysterium*, by Morten Lauridsen/H. Robert Reynolds; and *Irish Tune from County Derry*, by Percy Aldridge Grainger. ➤●

# Clap and Stomp Your Way to a More Responsive Band

*Lawrence Stoffel*

Among the many skills that students develop in rehearsals is the ability to watch and respond to a conductor's gestures. Getting students to actually watch a conductor is an enormous task in and of itself. When you add reading music, attending to playing posture, using proper technique, matching pitch with others, and blending together, this task becomes increasingly difficult. So can we expect students to also react to the specific gestures being used by the conductor? Yes, but as with any skill, it takes some practice to achieve good results.

**INGREDIENTS:**
No instruments; no music. Students are seated in their regular rehearsal rows of chairs.

**SERVES:**
Large ensembles utilizing a conductor.

If I notice my students not watching my conducting gestures, I will first ask myself, "Am I showing them anything to actually see? Am I using gestures that attempt to tell them something about how to play the music?" If students are not watching the conductor, most often it is because the conductor is not showing anything to actually watch! Unfortunately, if such conditions persist, students actually become trained to *not* watch the conductor.

To encourage students to watch the conductor and to reinvigorate the meaningfulness of my own conducting gestures, I will sometimes start a rehearsal with a "Hand Clapping and Foot Stomping" etude.

Divide the band into two equal halves—half of the band to your left and half of the band to your right. Tell the students only these instructions: To the left half say, "You will clap your hands." To the right side say, "You will stomp your feet." It is important to say nothing else, even if a student should ask a question. From this point, you communicate only with your hand, arm, and facial gestures.

Start with the half of the band who are hand clappers. Give them a simple downbeat gesture. At least one or two of the students will likely clap their hands together. Give a positive gesture to those students who did actually clap—a nod, a smile, or thumbs up. Give the downbeat again. Most of the students will now clap in reaction to your downbeat gesture (now two consecutive downbeats, then three, and then four). Elicit the same from the foot stompers. Should a clapper clap when the gesture was given to the stompers, react appropriately—a surprised look, a quick shake of the head, a shrug of the left hand to imply, "No, not you; that's for the stompers only." Return to the foot stompers, and take them through a short rhythmic pattern using again only arm gestures.

Return back to the clappers. Add gestures to communicate loud and soft dynamics. Change the rebound of your arm gestures to elicit heavy (pesante) and light (leggiero). Return back to the stompers, and do the same.

As the students become more confident in the exercise and more enthusiastic about the game, become more daring in your gestures: clap-clap-clap~stomp!~clap-clap~stomp!~clap-stomp-clap-stomp-stomp-stomp. Have the claps loud (forte) while the stomps are soft (piano), and then reverse the dynamic scheme. Have the clappers maintain a piano clapping tremolo (rapid pattering as fast as possible), while dictating a loud rhythmic pattern with the foot stompers. While the hand clappers and foot stompers are both tremolo, crescendo with the clappers and diminuendo with the stompers—then reverse the dynamics.

Students never fail to laugh when I lead them into the Queen hit song, "We Will Rock You" rhythm. I will always start it slowly at first so no one sees it coming, but gradually the tempo increases until the catchy ostinato is recognized by all: "stomp~~~~stomp~~~~~~clap~~~~~~~~~~stomp~~~~~stomp~~~~~~~~~~clap~~~~~~~~~~stomp~stomp~~~~clap~stomp-stomp-clap~stomp-stomp-clap . . . "

Over time, students will respond very discretely to subtle differences in your gestures. The size, speed/momentum, angle, direction, rebound, shape of hand, spread of fingers, angle of arms, and broadness of shoulders will all affect how the students execute each and every clap and stomp. Set up simple rhythmic patterns, and then follow up with seemingly random rhythms. Have two different rhythmic ideas juxtaposed between the clappers and stompers.

Listen to subtle differences in the way your students clap and stomp when you vary your gestures. Go from using a fist, to spread fingers ("jazz hands"), to index finger-to-thumb ("okay"), to heavy metal thumb and pinky finger extended, to traffic cop flat hand-style "stop," to fingers tense in a claw shape. And vary your arm positions—palms up, palms down, as if hugging a large tree trunk, a karate chop, a fist pump into the air. The variety of hand and arm positions and movements is limited only by your imagination (the same for your myriad facial expressions). Use both traditional conducting gestures and non-traditional gestures. Sometimes use a baton and other times, don't.

If you don't hear a difference in the way the students clap and stomp after showing a different gesture, then reiterate your gesture more emphatically. Let the students know with a disproving look that the clap or stomp needs to match your gestures, and show the gesture again. Get the students to *respond* to your differences in gestures. But remember, the key to developing students' attentiveness is to not talk! Let your gestures do the "talking."

Over time and repeated use of these exercises, your students will develop their ability to respond to your conducting gestures while playing their instruments. I also find that my own conducting skills improve after these exercises, as I am expanding my own repertory of conducting gestures. ➡●

# It's the Chef that Counts (Or: What's Making that Band Sound So Good?)

*Carl Strommen*

**INGREDIENTS:**
Desire. Dedication. Focus.

**SERVES:**
Players and listeners of all ages.

There is no question that the "ingredients" necessary to produce a successful band program are as critical as putting together a great meal. The back room of the restaurant, that team in the kitchen, is an appropriate metaphor for building a strong performing organization.

All band directors know what those ingredients are: the "meat and potatoes" (practice, more practice, lessons, sectionals, that very precious rehearsal time, technique development, etc.), and the "spice" (focus, desire, dedication)—all of which prepare the player to make it through what has to be one of the most complicated and intricate of team activities.

Yet, experience tells me that something else is in the pot, that elusive hint of flavor that pulls the whole meal together. So what is this intangible ingredient? Why is Band A more musical than Band B when they both share similar circumstances (*ingredients*, if you will)? Why did that band I just adjudicated from a rural district with meager resources perform at a musically superior level to the next competitor from a suburban area with obvious advantages?

It's the chef. Years of being involved with performing organizations at all levels has convinced me that despite whatever shortcomings or advantages a group suffers or enjoys, it all boils down (no pun intended) to the cook—the conductor. The passion of the person up front will drive and motivate the players. The ingredients may be there to a greater or lesser degree, but unless there is the love of music, that "fire in the belly" that is felt by the players and inspires and moves them, the group will be less than its potential. No matter what you dump in the pot, in the long run, it's all about the chef. ➡

# Developing a Philosophy for Success

*James Swearingen*

It is virtually impossible to be successful in the field of education without having formulated a personal teaching philosophy. This philosophy, based on a lifetime of personal experiences and observations, should serve as the foundation for your ability to achieve success. It should be noted that not every teacher selects music as his or her subject matter. What all teachers do share however, is the wonderful opportunity to include "lessons of life" as part of their daily classes. Therefore, what you value as being important, and what you believe in, should certainly be a reflection of your approach to teaching both music and the commonly accepted ideals of citizenship.

## INGREDIENTS:

Start by observing others in the profession, and whenever possible, learn from the best role models/master teachers available. Also, be prepared to encounter a few people that may provide you with the unique opportunity to learn how *not* to do something. Every experience, good or bad, will be a valuable tool for learning.

Anything of worth takes time. The nurturing of your philosophy may take several years to fully develop. Some teachers find it much easier to settle early on for mediocrity; however, be assured that the pot of gold at the end of the rainbow will be well worth the time invested.

You must have the ability to clearly articulate and communicate your philosophy. Strengthening your verbal and writing skills will help to ensure credibility amongst administrators, pupils, and parents.

You need to be the role model of your own philosophy if you expect others to follow your lead. Enough said!

When necessary, be prepared to make changes in your philosophy. Don't be afraid to try something different. Remove yourself from your comfort zone and embrace the opportunity for change. Remember, every old tradition once started out as a new and fresh idea.

## SERVES:

All dedicated music educators. All dedicated music students.

## BLEND WELL FOR A SUCCESSFUL PHILOSOPHY.

**An outstanding music class starts with an outstanding teacher.** Teaching, in and of itself, is an art that affords the wonderful opportunity to engage students. As a result, the educational attitude that is reflected in front of the class will have a tremendous effect on the success or failure of the teacher's instructional time. Should we then be surprised that when asked to describe their favorite teachers, the majority of people focused on humanistic qualities such as passion, humor, fairness, joy, dedication—and not subject matter?

> Your students won't care how much you know until they know how much you care.

**An outstanding music class starts with an outstanding musician.** A thorough knowledge of music, as it pertains to musical performance and awareness, is an attribute that every music instructor should possess.

**An outstanding music class is well organized and planned in advance.** Avoid doing your homework in front of the class.

> Failing to plan means you are planning to fail.

**An outstanding music class can be achieved if your "people" skills will allow you to relate to your students in a highly positive and constructive manner.**

> I've come to the frightening conclusion that I am the decisive element in the classroom. It is my personal approach that creates the climate. It is my daily mood that makes the weather. As a teacher I possess a tremendous power to make a child's life miserable or joyous. I can be a tool of torture or an instrument of inspiration. —Haim Ginott, noted child psychologist and teacher  ➥

# The Wonderful Complexities of Quality Repertoire

*John A. Thomson*

**INGREDIENTS:**

Repertoire selection for an ensemble is one of the most important choices a conductor makes during the year. The repertoire becomes the curriculum for that ensemble.

**SERVES:**

All instrumental students.

The most obvious consideration when selecting repertoire for an ensemble is the literature's suitability for the musical and technical sophistication of the ensemble. When reviewing a score for its appropriateness, consider its technical and rhythmic demands, instrumentation, ranges, scoring, and solo expectations. The conductor should compare these performance issues with the strengths and weaknesses of the ensemble.

While it is important to challenge an ensemble technically, it is not wise for a conductor to choose only music that is at the difficult edge of an ensemble's technical frontier. If a group always performs works at or beyond the limits of their ability, the students will only have time to think about technical production. A work that an ensemble can handle readily from a technical standpoint will give the students the opportunity to grow by focusing on aspects of music other than just getting the notes. Choose some repertoire at the ensemble's upper technical limits and other selections that are playable with a little bit of practice. Music that can be grasped more quickly offers the opportunity to play expressively with good tone, phrasing, intonation, balance, and blend. Remember, technique is a means to musical expression, not an end in itself.

Aside from the issues of difficulty and complexity, an ensemble's repertoire should include only the highest quality literature selected from the broadest historical base possible. Beginning with transcriptions, explore compositions from all historical periods up to and including contemporary and experimental works that stretch the ensemble's knowledge of modern styles.

Students should have the opportunity to learn and perform the master works of the medium that have stood the test of time. Certainly the profession should continue to encourage new works and listen eagerly to the latest compositions by our contemporary composers, but a primary expectation for each conductor should be to look back and decide what is the best music in the repertoire and to perform these masterworks on a regular or rotational basis. These are the works students should be exposed to as part of becoming musically literate.

Select literature with varied structures and textures. The challenge for conductors is to select quality literature with varied structures, forms, and textures, while avoiding those works that follow a cookie-cutter formula. Look for creative and interesting scoring ideas that sound fresh and innovative. By the way, don't neglect slower works that emphasize legato cantabile playing. The students will learn to play well-crafted musical lines and concerts will be refreshed with the change-of-pace programming.

Finally, select a few works each year as a means of teaching musical concepts, what some music educators call the unit-study approach to curriculum. A set of lesson plans can be centered on these exemplar compositions as a way for students to learn more about the music than just their assigned parts. Include biographical information about the composer, a brief explanation of the form and compositional devices in the work, as well as appropriate vocabulary that is necessary to understand the work. Not every piece has to be studied this intensely, but all selected works should stand up to the tests of having significant form, an important historical perspective, and a fresh and unique approach. Although such criteria make it a difficult task to find and select quality repertoire, the knowledge students gain from each new work will inevitably carry over to the next piece they study. Common strands of knowledge are present in each fine composition, and it is the process of introducing students to these wonderful complexities that makes teaching so exciting.

# The Most Important Hour of the Day

*Johnnie Vinson*

There are obviously not enough hours in the teaching day to do everything we would like to do in order improve our ensembles. However, in terms of the success of our groups, the rehearsal is *the most important hour of the day.* If the rehearsal is effective, the ensemble has a much better chance of being successful.

**INGREDIENTS:**
Organization, attention to detail, thorough planning, and the careful carrying out of the rehearsal plan.

**SERVES:**
All instrumental ensembles.

I've often joked that the surest way to make an ensemble serious is to dress them up and put them in front of an audience! Think how much better our ensembles would be if students would rehearse with the same intensity and care demonstrated at concerts. Although directors often expect or hope that their ensembles will perform better in concert than they do in rehearsal, experience shows that the opposite is probably true. Performance anxiety can cause a variety of problems (rushing tempos, insecure intonation, atypical balance and blend) that do not normally occur in rehearsal. If an ensemble does actually perform better in concert, the probable reason is that the players are more focused and are making a better effort than they do in a normal rehearsal.

If we really want to have successful performances, then we must have successful rehearsals. In terms of our ensemble's success, the rehearsal is the most important hour of the day. We should have a definite plan for every rehearsal and we should implement that plan.

For a rehearsal to be successful, the director must first have the attention of the students. Secondly, the students must be making a genuine effort to improve. These two factors are extremely important!

The director should ask the following questions about his or her rehearsals. Is there an appropriate warm-up and is the director with the ensemble during the warm-up? Is the music worthwhile? Is the music challenging to the strong players, yet accessible to the weaker ones? What musical details are to be rehearsed? Are most the students playing most of the time? Is the group focused on the task at hand? Is the ensemble accomplishing something during the rehearsal?

We should have specific objectives in mind for each rehearsal and should have a plan for attaining these objectives. Effective rehearsals don't happen by chance. Careful planning of rehearsals and carrying out of these plans are essential. Consider the following suggestions:

1.  Chairs and music stands should be set up before the students arrive for rehearsal and all music to be rehearsed should be in the folders. Setting up the band or passing out music as the rehearsal begins wastes valuable rehearsal time and creates a chaotic atmosphere in the room.

2.  List the order of music to be rehearsed on the chalkboard or whiteboard, and insist that students have their music in order. While the wind players warm up, the percussion section should get organized and ready to rehearse.

3.  Start on time. Even five wasted minutes at the beginning of each rehearsal adds up to many wasted hours over the course of the school year.

4.  Have a student assistant take attendance by empty chairs. Don't waste rehearsal time calling roll. A student assistant should also handle phone calls, messages, etc., during rehearsal.

5.  Place a pencil in every music folder and require students to mark their parts with the conductor's instructions. If something is worth stopping for, it's worth marking.

6.  Work the difficult parts of the music early in the rehearsal, after warm-up and tuning, while the students' concentration is best.

7.  When preparing for festival or contest, have students number the measures in their parts. This will save a lot of rehearsal time over several weeks. ("Let's start at measure 54," instead of "Let's start 14 measures after letter C.")

8.  The conductor must have a mental concept of how the music would sound if played perfectly. The ensemble's playing should be constantly evaluated and compared to this mental image of perfection. Then, the conductor should give the ensemble feedback to gradually mold their performance toward this image of perfection.

9.  Each stop during rehearsal should be used for giving specific instructions. Little is achieved with comments such as, "You're out of tune . . . you must play in tune." Even less is accomplished with the philosophy, "Let's play it through again and hope it gets better."

10. Don't spend an excessive amount of rehearsal time talking to the group. This results in the students becoming restless and inattentive. The conductor's comments should be brief, concise, and related to the music. Have as many of the students as possible playing most of the time.

11. Insist on maximum concentration on the part of the students; the better the focus, the better the rehearsal. Little, if anything, can be accomplished in the midst of chaos.

12. End rehearsals playing something the students like. This generates enthusiasm for the next rehearsal.

13. After rehearsal, go through your scores and make written notes concerning what you want to do at the next rehearsal, while it's still fresh on your mind. Also, keep a written record of what you rehearse every day in order to balance the time spent on the various selections in the folder.

14. Once the music begins to sound good to you, record rehearsals about once a week. Evaluate the recording and make notes for the next rehearsal.

There are obviously not enough hours in the teaching day to do everything we would like to improve our ensembles. However, in terms of the success of our groups, the rehearsal is *the most important hour of the day.* If the rehearsal is effective, the ensemble has a much better chance of being successful! ➤

# Times Have Changed: How About Your Warm-up?

*Barry Ward*

Today, it may be increasingly difficult to find students with competent instrumental technique within the ranks of young musicians. In general, students are performing music carefully selected and at the correct grade level and created by composers and publishers who are providing works of musical diversity. But, is this abundance of carefully orchestrated music just part of a larger problem? Remember the "old days" when we all had to *play up* in the level of musical difficulty? And how about those transcriptions for developing technique! Additionally, there have been many recent changes in academic demands, additional extra-curricular activities, and computer "entertainment." Today's life style leaves little time for out-of-class practice and thus creates a need to spend more time during the rehearsal period developing technical skills.

## INGREDIENTS:
Hand out a circle of fourths grid sheet with major scales major. Apply general instrumental basics to a short list of exercises—a *Daily Basics Menu*. Start with small scale fragments and develop with variations in length, speed, and range. Modify the menu to more advanced levels with one- and two-octave scales in all keys.

## SERVES:
Individual, group, and full instrumental classes.

Diagnosing the *illness* (lack of technique), of course, is just a first step. The next step, identifying and implementing a *remedy*, is more difficult. This requires rehearsal time and necessitates that warm-up time be a well-organized, systematic approach to technical development. It demands a methodology that is flexible yet precise enough to target basic performance goals.

First, in order to include all students at all levels, it is very important to emphasize good performance fundamentals, coupled with advancing techniques on a frequent schedule. The topics and individual exercises can be creatively controlled with each exercise having a specific purpose. Generic titles such as "good air," "faster fingers," "faster tonguing" or "lip flexibility," and a "wider range" help determine a list of topics to be developed. This short list of exercises is a *Daily Basics Menu*. As these stylized exercises are continually developed with increased length, speed, and a widening range, scale practice should be introduced, utilizing the circle of fourths. Any length scale fragment can be easily doubled in length and tempo, hence the use of a shortened term, "double-double," meaning both variables are doubled. Long tones, for example, may be doubled in length, or one-octave scales may instantly become two octaves and performed with a variety of rhythm patterns, articulations, and tempos. Consequently, technique develops around the circle of fourths at an exponential speed.

Finally, each daily menu builds upon itself with exercises containing a comprehensive review of old material and the possible introduction of carefully selected new material. At each point the teacher must carefully evaluate the level of future assignments. Mastery of basic performance skills, combined with comprehensive scale and interval performance, act as a beacon or guiding light. The following rationale for developing comprehensive technique at the beginning and intermediate levels may be used as a course syllabus or other descriptive document:

---

Good performance results can be achieved from a well-organized and creative warm-up. Exercises may be improvised that will emphasize instrumental basics. Beginning students, for example, are started with a supplemental worksheet, a single sheet with on-the-spot exercises. These exercises can be easily altered at the next lesson or kept the same. Younger students enjoy labeling each exercise with descriptive titles such as the "longest note ever," "the finger roller coaster," or "the tongue "twister," which results in more personal involvement.

By keeping the basics menu system intact, most instrumentalists make quick transitions to more advanced levels. At some point the teacher may choose to introduce the circle of fourths for comprehensive scale development. Almost all instrumentalists do best when presented with a printed scales grid that illustrates scales around the circle of fourths.

Scale grids visually facilitate the introduction of scale performance in full or fragmented form. Three- or five-note scale fragments, for example, offer a user-friendly approach to learning exercises in all keys, possibly even before a full scale has been learned. Moreover, these scale grids, coupled with a menu of stylized exercises, offer great flexibility with precise micro and macro performance goals. Just think: the vast amount of material offered in method books may be studied from a single printed scales grid!

A well-designed series of menus will offer students a systematic review and introduce new material. Certainly all students will benefit from basic instruction; however, in this case the flexibility to jump ahead to more challenging material can offer increased interest and enthusiasm. In fact, once all scales have been learned, the real value in this approach may be the linkage to other established methods.

---

Of course, developing a well-organized warm-up period takes time and planning. From basic exercises organized by menu, to the use of a printed scales grid ranging from scale fragments to full scales, the total focus should be a personal approach to technical development. The entire process focuses on specific goals selected by the teacher in real time. What more could be asked from an organized system of technical development? Whatever warm-up material you select, it is important to understand that times have changed, as have students' daily schedules. Daily warm-ups must reflect today's changing times. ➤●

# Developing Solid Teaching Skills

*Renee Westlake*

Did you know that a good teacher is kind of like a sturdy three-legged stool? I had a three-legged step stool when I was younger. It was the sturdiest piece of furniture in my house. It never rocked, it never wobbled, and it could hold a great deal of weight! One day I was using it incorrectly and had placed it upside down. One of my family members didn't see it there and tripped over it, breaking one of the legs in half. It's hard to stand on two legs of a three-legged stool, just like it's hard to be a good teacher if any of the ingredients are missing.

**INGREDIENTS:**
1. **Competence.** A master music teacher must have knowledge, skills, and experience indigenous to his or her field.
   a. Musicianship is a critical component in the competence of a music teacher. An understanding of tone quality, phrasing, pulse, rhythmic subdivision, reading, and musical expression contributes to passing that information along to students. Applying that understanding to performance enhances student learning greatly.
   b. Problem solving is another skill of the master teacher. Every day in education holds surprises and a need for flexibility. A problem solver does not become overwhelmed and burned out by these unexpected events.
   c. Researching resources gives the competent teacher that extra advantage in the quest for excellence. Knowing who to ask, where to look, what is available, and when to search: all are intrinsically linked to being fully competent.
2. **Organization**. I have known many creative teachers who are random and abstract by nature. The master teacher figures out how to master the completion of concrete tasks, even when anticipating all the details isn't something they come by naturally.
   a. Plan your classes and rehearsals, even if you fly well by the seat of your pants! Creating an outline saves time. When teaching is planned, important points are not forgotten. Include pacing, motivating activities, challenge, tension and release, and educational closure. Doing this helps students want to learn in your class.
   b. Prioritize your day. Most teachers cannot do everything there is to be done. Give yourself a set time to answer phone calls and e-mails. Schedule time to file music, set up your room, and attend to proactive planning that ensures successful performances.
   c. Delegate! Train students and parents to be leaders. They benefit and you save your sanity. There are so many details having to do with paperwork, room cleanup, uniform checkout, and event planning that others can be trained to do. It takes a little longer the first time, but it gets easier.

3. **Interpersonal skills.** If you set others up for success, support them, take an interest in them, and really care—you are well on your way to being a master teacher.
   a. Care! You have to love what you do and like people. I am reminded of an article I read awhile back in the *NFHS Music Journal* titled, "How Can You Be Burned Out When You Were Never On Fire?" As this title suggests, it's critical to stay fired up.
   b. Listen! Call parents once in a while when their child shows some improvement. Go to a student's soccer game. Have a potluck dinner for helper parents. Listen to others' ideas and dreams and incorporate them into your own dreams.
   c. Praise! Give others credit for their part in your students' successes; in turn, they will give you credit for being a master teacher.

**SERVES:**
All educators who aspire to make a difference in the lives of their students.

Our students, parents, administrators, and community count on us to make the core course of music what it needs to be to provide the necessary balance in our students' total education. Remember the three-legged stool? In the same way that this stool cannot stand if one of the legs is missing, a teacher cannot be a master of his or her craft if one of the three *ingredients* is missing.

We all have a leg of our own stool that needs repair now and then. Whether you are seeking to improve your competence, your organization, or your interpersonal communication skills, a great way to equip your toolbox (or recipe book!) to make the needed reparations is to attend professional development sessions and conferences at every opportunity. You will rediscover the energy, motivation, skill, and vision that will help you ably restore the balance you need to perform at the master level of your craft. ➤●

# Solving Rhythm Problems in the Instrumental Ensemble

*Garwood Whaley*

Rhythm is the primary musical element found in all music from all historical periods. It is also the most problematic. Why then is rhythm so often neglected as a daily component of band and orchestra rehearsals? Totally neglected? Of course not, but it is usually addressed only when problems occur and, then, not as a regular part of rehearsal strategies.

**INGREDIENTS:**
Rhythm sheet handouts or rhythm book (without pitches—just rhythms and rests). Make sure that the materials cover all rhythm problems that will be contained in music played during the year. Clap and count out loud at the beginning of every rehearsal. Consistency is essential.

**SERVES:**
All instrumental and voice students.

Dealing with rhythm problems piece-by-piece is frustrating and redundant. Teaching a difficult rhythm by rote may solve the problem in one piece but, most often, the ability to play the same rhythm in another piece does not transfer. Rote teaching of rhythms is a *band-aid approach* that does nothing for long-term learning. Like any musical skill, teaching rhythm requires regular application and must become a daily part of every rehearsal. Combining rhythm training with playing an instrument does not work as effectively as isolating rhythm alone. In other words, isolate rhythm by clapping and counting out loud using a standard counting system. The focus must be on pure rhythm, without having to deal with tone production, intonation, or articulation.

Try this. At the beginning of every rehearsal, using either rhythm sheets or a rhythm book, have students count out loud using a standard counting system as they clap the rhythms. (I use Basics in Rhythm published by Meredith Music Publications). Begin with simple rhythms and progress to more difficult examples during the school year. Try to complete one page each day. Insist that students count out loud, since over time, they will develop the ability to hear the counting syllables in their mind. After establishing rhythm training as a normal part of each rehearsal (two or three weeks), complete the rhythm drill for the day by transferring the exercise to playing on a unison pitch. Stress the need to count mentally while playing. From that time on, after clapping each exercise, play the rhythms on a unison pitch while counting silently.

Assessment is important. At the end of each week or at the conclusion of a rhythm unit of multiple pages, have each student demonstrate their mastery by clapping and counting a few measures from the unit during a designated rehearsal. This takes very little time, since each student is only performing several measures. If a student cannot clap and count the excerpt successfully, work with the student individually until he or she is up to speed.

By taking a proactive approach to solving rhythm problems before they occur, you will provide students with a long-term comprehensive approach to decoding rhythms on their own; improvement will be almost instant. And, thanks to their ability to recognize rhythms with the help of rhythmic syllablization, students will be able to transfer their newfound skills from piece to piece. A byproduct will be the improvement in sight-reading skills, leading to more productive rehearsals and a potential increase in acceptance to regional and district ensembles. As a teacher, you can be reassured that this approach will provide students with concepts and skills that will take them far beyond their school years. Their ability to problem solve and perform independently throughout their adult lives fulfills the true goal of music education. ➤

# Delicious Dot!

*Carol Zeisler*

**INGREDIENTS:**
Musician. "My Country 'Tis of Thee" or any musical selection containing dotted rhythms.

**SERVES:**
Beginning students, intermediate students, advanced students? Students who have never had a private teacher.

**Preparation:**
Can be done in 24 seconds, 24 minutes, or 24 hours in advance.

**Serving Suggestions:**
Stir before serving. Serves three equal or unequal judges. Take your dotted notes and slice them into three equal parts. Stir into any meal.

The answer is 3.
The question is . . . What does a dot equal?

The answer is, half the value of the note that it follows.
The question is . . . What is the rule for the dot?

The answer is, subdivide the dotted note?
The question is . . . What is another approach to counting?

Let's play Jeopardy. (*do do, do do, do do do* . . . ) The category is *the dot*.

A. The answer is three half notes.
Q. What does a dotted whole note equal?

A. The answer is three quarter notes.
Q. What does a dotted half note equal?

A. The answer is three eighth notes.
Q. What does a dotted quarter note equal?

A. The answer is three sixteenth notes.
Q. What does a dotted eighth note equal?

A. The answer is three thirty-second notes.
Q. What does a dotted sixteenth note equal?

    *Ding, ding, ding! Double Jeopardy question!*

A. The answer is 3.
Q. What is the magic number?

**Vocal version:**
> My Country 'tis 'tis 'tis of thee,
> Sweet land of lib lib lib erty, of thee I sing sing sing.
> Land where my fa fa fa thers died, land of our pil pil pil grim's pride,
> from every moun moun moun tainside, let freedom ring ring ring.

**Instrumental version:**
- Side dish can be served with any musical preparation.
- Any time you have a dotted note, slice and dice. (Play the subdivision).
- Remember, the magic number is 3.
- Subdivide the beat and watch the true value of the dot make your ears water.

**Note:** Serve only in rehearsal. ➤●

# Clarinets, an Essential Ingredient to a Well-Prepared Ensemble

*Dennis Zeisler*

Bands today have severe balance problems, due to a lack of clarinets. Often times, there are as many trumpets in an ensemble as there are clarinets. As a general rule, an ensemble should have a minimum of three clarinets per trumpet to maintain proper ensemble balance and timbre. The more clarinets an ensemble has, the warmer or darker the sound will be. Don't forget the low clarinets, bass and contralto, as they help add to the bass line in the ensemble.

**INGREDIENTS:**

**Good instruments.** Students should be encouraged to purchase a name brand clarinet with a good mouthpiece. Try any of the Selmer, Buffet, Leblanc, or Yamaha clarinets, as there is one to fit any budget. While a wooden clarinet is highly desirable, plastic and composite instruments are also well made and can be used by students through high school.

**Mouthpiece.** It is important to have all students purchase the same mouthpiece for a uniform and consistent sound. I recommend the Vandoren B45 mouthpiece as one that is always consistent. It is a medium open mouthpiece (distance of the reed to the mouthpiece) and works well with any brand instrument.

**Reeds.** Students should use a medium strength reed somewhere around a 3. For younger students, Rico, Rico Royal, LaVoz, and Mitchell Laurie reeds are fine and affordable. For more advanced students, there are many professional-level reeds, but quite often they need to be adjusted.

**Other equipment.** Ligature and barrels should be recommended by a private teacher as there are many available and they can be costly.

**SERVES:**

All clarinet players.

Take all of the above ingredients and combine them into a section. Developing a strong clarinet section will make any ensemble sound better. It is important for the director to work alone with the clarinets, including the low clarinets, as they should constitute the largest section of the band. First start with the sound the clarinet players are producing. What is *their* model? What is *your* model? A great deal of air should be going through the mouthpiece to keep the reed vibrating. This will help to even out the tone and range, especially the high notes.

As with any wind instrument, first make sure that proper diaphragmatic breathing is being used. Next, begin by playing slow chorales or *Treasury of Scales* to balance the soprano and low clarinets. This will give each player a chance to listen to his or her own part and make a decision about balance. Once balance is achieved, it is essential that each part—first, second, third, and bass—all work to blend tone and pitch. Start with the ears of the teacher until the players can hear on their own. Using a tuner is important at first, but you are really trying to develop the player's ability to listen and make musical decisions. Once the section understands the expectations of tone, pitch, balance, and blend, through the guidance of the teacher (band director), the principal player can handle the sectional rehearsal.

When each section has worked out pitch, balance, and blend, you are ready to add your essential ingredient to the ensemble: the clarinet section! Listen carefully to how much better your band sounds with enough clarinets to balance with the trumpets. Listen to how many inner lines you now hear that before went unheard because of weak second, third, and bass clarinet parts.

With proper clarinet representation, your musical recipe is complete! Enjoy! ━●

# Notes

# Notes

# Notes

# Notes

# Notes

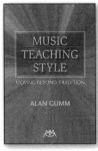

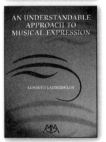